THE ROCK MUSICIAN

$\mathcal{T}$HE $\mathcal{R}$OCK

EDITED BY

TONY SCHERMAN

ST. MARTIN'S PRESS

NEW YORK

$\mathcal{M}$USICIAN

Photograph of George Clinton by Ebet Roberts; Paul McCartney: Ebet Roberts; Bruce Springsteen: James Shive/Retna Ltd.; Bono: Ebet Roberts; Marvin Gaye: Ebet Roberts; Prince: Ebet Roberts; Chrissie Hynde: Ebet Roberts; John Lydon: Ebet Roberts; Guns N' Roses: George Bodnar/Retna Ltd.; Allman Brothers: Bob Gruen/Star File; Stevie Ray Vaughan: Ebet Roberts; Earl Palmer: Rick Malkin.

Design by Judith A. Stagnitto

Library of Congress Cataloging-in-Publication Data

The Rock musician / edited by Tony Scherman.
    p. cm.
Interviews and profiles originally published in *Musician* magazine.
ISBN 0-312-09502-3 (pbk.).—ISBN 0-312-09501-5 (hc)
    1. Rock musicians. I. Scherman, Tony. II. *Musician* (Gloucester, Mass.)
ML385.R74 1993
781.66'092'2—dc20
                                    94-10637
                                        CIP
                                        MN

First Edition: August 1994
10 9 8 7 6 5 4 3 2 1

Contents

F O R E W O R D

Truly, we live in dark times! The empire of easy reading spreads its tentacles wider and wider, snuffing out all that is spontaneous, curious, serious, or subversive.

I started writing for *Musician* because I had a writer's curiosity about people and a musician's curiosity about how music is made. I was never a "rock critic"; I wanted to describe how musicians think, work, and live. There was really only one place I could do that, at least on a regular basis and for money that wasn't a total insult (if it didn't always come on time; as I write this, I'm reminded that Bill Flanagan owes me $700—no, *$1,300,* counting my writer's cut for stories in this book and the companion *The Jazz Musician.* Anthologized colleagues: Keep on Flanagan's back about this!).

Of course, *Musician* is not free from the pressures of the market: from pain-in-the-ass advertisers, from a recession which, casting its depressing cloud over my entire stay as staff editor, resulted in safer stories and a constant, debilitating anxiety over the cover. Trying to orchestrate and negotiate a commercially viable cover story, watching it fall through, brainstorming another, having that fall through, facing a looming ship-date with no cover story at all (for the fourth straight month) when publishing wisdom dictates the do-or-die, absolute, white-knuckles necessity of a hot, sexy cover—when *only* such a cover will put the issue securely into the black and maybe begin to salvage another so-so year—well, no wonder Bill Flanagan has begun to behave erratically.

So if ours are a new Dark Ages and it's up to a dedicated few to keep lit the candles of honesty, creativity, and bullshit detection, light a candle for poor *Musician.* Celebrate its lonely path, and pray that it holds its wayward, stubborn, enlightening, typo-ridden course for another twenty years.

TONY SCHERMAN
JUNE 1993

INTRODUCTION

Musician magazine was started in 1976, when pants were wide, sex was safe, and punk was just starting to raise its ugly head. *Musician* was a jazz magazine then, navigating the feuds between the purists and the forces of fusion, and offering a thoughtful alternative to the moldy-fig jazz publications of the day. Musicians took *Musician* seriously from the start, and before long some of the more serious rock players, fed up with what they saw as the irrelevance of the rock 'n' roll press, began wanting to talk to *Musician,* too.

Paul McCartney used *Musician* to break a ten-year silence on discussing the Beatles. Steely Dan, then the most reclusive rock stars, gave *Musician* two lengthy interviews. Joni Mitchell saw a chance to explain her detours away from pop to an audience that shared her vocabulary and values. Such access had its effect. By the early 1980s *Musician* was a smart rock magazine with regular jazz coverage, rather than a jazz magazine with occasional rock.

What *Musician* provided—what, as it creeps up on its twentieth year, it continues to provide—was a forum for players to talk about their creativity. Simple as that. Sometimes creativity comes as musical notes, sometimes as lyrics, sometimes as a philosophy, often with a history. *Musician* has tried to catch it however it came.

In the years since the magazine started, the communications industry has exploded. Once there were only two or three places someone could go to find out what Keith Richards or Pete Townshend had to say, and *Musician* was one of them. Now there are dozens, from MTV and "Entertainment Tonight" to *People* magazine and *USA Today*. But the explosion in the number of delivery systems seems to have been accompanied by a reduction in the attention span of each one. You can now find out what's new with Richards and Townshend in fifty different places—but only for thirty seconds each. *Musician* has remained the rare place where artists get a chance to talk at length, where there's still faith in the audience's attention span, and where we assume that the reader already has a lot of basic knowledge before we begin. Unlike most entertainment publications, we don't start every profile with the rocket leaving Krypton.

Musicians appreciate that—that's why they'll ask to talk to *Musician* while blowing off publications with far bigger circulations. Writers appreciate it, too—which is why the best rock journalists do their best work for us, despite the fact that we pay for a ten-thousand-word story only a little more than what *Vanity Fair* (for example) pays for a two-paragraph short. Everyone wants a chance to be taken seriously, to get their story told right.

All of which made it very tough to select twelve stories to represent the two thousand features *Musician* has published. We wanted a balance of different voices without creating a cacophony. Some of the subjects in this book are already history—Marvin Gaye and Stevie Ray Vaughan have died violent deaths since their *Musician* interviews. Prince quit giving interviews right after this one—it remains his most important statement. Earl Palmer and George Clinton are not as famous as those other musicians, but their contributions to America's creative heritage are at least as great. If you don't know why, these profiles will help you understand.

Paul McCartney, Bruce Springsteen, and U2 have maintained long relationships with the magazine—we selected these interviews because they caught those artists at moments of reflection, when their paths were turning and they weren't sure where they were going next.

Laughter is one of the main characteristics of the rocker's life, and the one most often left out of the writing about it. There are plenty of laughs in the pieces on Johnny Rotten and the Allman Brothers, which makes the darkness in their stories more striking. There's plenty of darkness in the stories of Guns N' Roses and the star-crossed Pretenders, which makes the humor in those profiles more welcome.

Someone once wrote that the defining characteristic of *Musician* magazine was that it assumed that a musician was a worthy thing to be. That's true; that is what the magazine's about. And also this: A musician is a complex thing to be. A musician must be like a painter or poet, creating his art in isolation. Then he has to shift hats and become a performer, selling his show to the crowd. A rock musician has one foot in the gallery and one in the circus, and if he is successful he is both revered and mocked out of all proportion. He has to be able to speak with one voice to the lonely woman lying in the dark listening to the stereo, and to the gang of boys in their car singing to the radio, and to the crowd cheering in the arena. Such dexterity demands a contradictory personality—few artists can maintain such balance for very long.

This book is about the ones who can.

BILL FLANAGAN
EDITOR, MUSICIAN
MAY 1993

THE ROCK
MUSICIAN

THE SERIOUS

METAFOOLISHNESS OF

FATHER FUNKADELIC,

GEORGE CLINTON

BY CHIP
STERN

In not-so-ancient incanta-

tions, alchemists, priests, and witch doctors have al-

lowed spirit forces to flow through them, inviting

disorder, mystery, the sensual, a sense of the infinite—

going all *the way out. In the chaos that lies beyond*

the gossamer fabrications of ego, the human race has

sensed the symbolic unity of nature and the cosmos—

in both the sacred and the profane. Such has been the

path of primitives and mystery cults throughout the

ages toward the creation of a mythology that reconciled heaven and earth.

Western civilization has not placed a premium on *magic*. Upon becoming the dominant religious force in Rome, Christianity immediately set out to clean house of all mystics, dissenters, and assorted freaks. The rise of the Roman Catholic Church was a triumph of the priestly over the prophetic, and in this highly institutionalized form there became only one accepted way to dig on Jesus. Any deviations were interpreted as heresy, sacrilege, madness, or a work of the devil—in those days, they'd burn your ass for falling out of line.

In the wake of the Great Schism and the catastrophic religious wars that raged across Europe in the sixteenth century, Western man decided to clean up *all* of his funk. The state became preeminent, allowing the church to co-exist as a lesser partner in exchange for its divine seal of approval. Newton postulated an orderly clockwork universe, and science henceforth pursued the grail of progress and provability. And industrialization brought on the worldwide dominance of the West. The bywords of Western man became *order* and *expediency*.

But in jettisoning his connections to magic, Western man threw out the baby with the bath. Little did he know that his house would collapse in the conflagration of the twentieth century, and that the funk would rise again.

Anytime someone wants to call me "Nigger," I give him the privilege, because only a Nigger could have gone through the things that we, the black people, have gone through and survived. So if you call me "Nigger," you only identify me as one of the strongest in the world. I feel like it's an honor, not a disgrace, to be called "Nigger." To me it tells me that I am the strongest. Only me and a beast of burden—such as an ox—could have subdued and survived. Anything else would have been extinct by now.

JOHNNY SHINES, *from* Blues *by*
Robert Neff and Anthony Connor

The worldview of the Africans who had the divine misfortune to end up in America was so substantially different from that of their masters that massa thought his slaves downright backward. But somehow the "savages" survived, and so did their African culture. In spite of the suppression of African roots, the essence went underground and persisted in many new garments.

In the black churches of the South, a meeting of Western and African music took place. In the call-and-response of the preacher and his congregation, the chanting litany of field hollers and work songs, and the hoodoo-voodoo of the back country, a musical vocabulary and tradition developed and "jes grew." At the risk of being simplistic, we can call this mutant musical form the blues.

After the Civil War, the first great exodus of blacks took place. Urban centers all over the United States suddenly had substantial black populations. In the future shock of the "big city," the blues took on many new forms. Ragtime became the rage, and minstrelsy was to have a profound effect on American humor and musical theater.

In his surrealistic historical fantasia *Mumbo Jumbo*, author Ishmael Reed reports serious outbreaks of the black plague known as "jes grew" in the 1890s and 1920s. Whereas most plagues cause decay and death, "jes grew" enlivened and delighted those who became afflicted with it; the most obvious symptoms were convulsive dancing and white people imitating blacks! Needless to say, the ruling class perceived that its basis for authority would be seriously undermined by "jes grew." The celestial high C that Louis Armstrong trumpeted on "West End Blues" was a shout heard round the world: "Jes grew" would not be denied.

The blues-based music that evolved over the next fifty years gave birth to two parallel streams: jazz and funk. Distinctions between these blues brothers revolve around their social uses. Jazz became an art music. Armstrong, Coleman Hawkins, and Earl Hines inaugurated a new age of virtuosity, Fletcher Henderson and Duke Ellington articulated an orchestral language, and Lester Young and Jo Jones developed a new melodic-rhythmic freedom with Count Basie that caused jazz to transcend its role as entertainment. The spiritual descendants of the swing era were the beboppers. At first, people were dancing to the jet-propelled new music, but as time passed, bop became less a dance music than music for the sake of music. With Coltrane, Coleman, Taylor, Dolphy, and Ayler, jazz became still more cerebral.

The music I'm calling funk developed along more functional lines. Boogie-woogie pianists and country bluesmen like Robert Johnson played a coarser music than their jazz brothers, but they were often more visceral and emotionally direct. In the swing-based jump of Louis Jordan, the barrelhouse rocking of Professor Longhair, and the electric urgency of Muddy Waters, the roots of rhythm and blues were sown. *R&B* is a catchall term to describe the music that people danced to in bars and heard on jukeboxes; it featured insistent backbeats, hollering vocals, chunky electric guitars and basses, wailing organs, stomping pianos, and honking horn sections. It was a joyous noise, and it emphasized the *entertainment* aspects jazzmen disdained. Add to this stew the influence of country music, popular vocal groups, and gospel singers, ignite it with

Elvis, and you've got rock 'n' roll—which unleashed a tidal wave of funk upon America in the 1950s.

Many of the symbols and images of funk were things derived from the black inner-city streets: processed hair, doo-wop, the stroll, diddy bopping, and lots of slang expressions and code words. The funk gave us people like Little Richard, Screamin' Jay Hawkins, Chuck Berry, Ray Charles, and James Brown. It even gave us funky jazzmen: Stanley Turrentine, Bobby Timmons, and Horace Silver, who reacted against the dreariness of West Coast cool jazz by dipping into their gospel roots. During the 1960s funk evolved into the soul sound of Motown and Memphis. By 1967, the expanded consciousness of the decade spawned the psychedelic era, commencing with *Sgt. Pepper* and leading in short order to the outer-space electric funk of Jimi Hendrix and Sly Stone. Hendrix and Sly had an incalculable effect on Miles Davis, whose *Bitches Brew* began the stampede of crossover jazz in the 1970s.

All of this passionate speculation is intended to give you some background as to why we have the Art Ensemble of Chicago and Parliament/Funkadelic coexisting on the cover of *Musician*. Both groups epitomize the evolution of the black urban experience in the 1970s: the Art Ensemble representing the cosmopolitan (jazz), and P-Funk representing the street (funk). Their approaches differ—one is cerebral and the other visceral—but both groups share the central element of *magic*.

Both are tribal in that strong individuals subsume their personalities in a communal ideal; both employ theater, humor, and ceremony in the invocation of a myth; both deal in the resolution of opposites, chaos and order; and, most important, both dangle the best elements of the blues tradition in the face of an overwhelming commercial regression called disco.

Disco has become the new ballroom dancing of the seventies. There is no individuality to disco dancing, no room for you to do your own dance and really freak. While writing this story, I saw a disco version of "Yankee Doodle Dandy" on "The Lawrence Welk Show." In the face of such a frightening cultural consensus, the Art Ensemble of Chicago and Parliament/Funkadelic assert the hegemony of rhythm: one through a pancultural synthesis, the other through the power of uncut funk.

In today's disco-ized world, Parliament/Funkadelic offers *the great alternative stream of syncopation in funk*, a music so rich in contrapuntal design, going in so many directions at once, that it signifies a journey through the African and American past into a universal future. George Clinton and Parliament/Funkadelic have the Mothership all toked up and their funk is pointed toward the stars. To find out where the U.S. Funk Mob comes from, and where they intend to take us, we must visit the laboratory of Dr. Funkenstein himself.

THE MOTHERSHIP

United Sound in Detroit is located in a bright blue building nestled innocuously among fraternity houses and teaching centers on the campus of Wayne State University. Little would one suspect that inside this humble-looking building were hatched the greatest of the early Motown hits. Inside the labyrinth of little offices and rehearsal spaces is a high-ceilinged room, the main recording studio. Seated at the computerized space station mixing board are a recording engineer and William "Bootsy" Collins himself. Bootsy is calmly sucking on a lemon while supervising the first product for the Funk Mob's new label, Uncle Jam Records.

Clinton arrives shortly thereafter, an elflike figure with bright darting eyes, an unruly mat of red kinky hair, a lopsided grin, and garish Captain America boots. He is obviously the man in charge, but he carries his authority in a casual, friendly manner, acting more like referee than corporate magnate. Looking through an issue of a soul magazine featuring a story on his group, Clinton chuckles over an interview with Sly Stone. "Sheeeeeit, Sly raps better than most cats write lyrics—all it needs is a backbeat."

Clinton's mind shoots in several directions at once; in the next instant he is discussing calling up James Brown to set up a collaboration with the godfather of funk.

"This is the type of thing they say can't be done; too much ego or somethin' like that. But I don't care whose record it appears on, or what label. Don't make no difference to me. What counts is that every time someone plugs in, it helps the nation. That's what the Mothership Connection is all about—connecting all those people who've been disconnected.

"All we got to do is lay the rhythm tracks here at United Sound, and I can record the other tracks anywhere in the world. Because this particular room has that sound that hits you right *on* your primal button. And people be thinking, 'What does that remind me of?' and they don't connect that subliminally they're hearing that old Motown sound on the bottom in this room."

At the time Motown was starting to make waves, the founding members of the vocal group the Parliaments—George Clinton, Fuzzy Haskins, Grady Thomas, Calvin Simon, and Ray Davis—ran a barbershop in Plainfield, New Jersey. They'd do a good process, sell a little reefer out the back, and after hours they'd smoke, drink a little wine, and harmonize doo-wops. The allure of Motown finally became too much for the Parliaments to bear, so they sold the barbershop, bought a van, and headed to Detroit, where they camped out in front of Motown. The group got an audition, which led to a songwriting contract for Clinton.

"I think there was a craving in the black music at the time—Motown probably being the best—for melody and lyrical things, that was probably wooed on by the success of the pop music. A lot of the blues thing slipped away, and things got so sophisticated that the rhythms became straight and predictable, and the lyrics and melody became more important, because without all of that rhythm and syncopation, you could do the melody clearer. All of that took place at Motown; the syncopation left off for a minute, and it became something cool that everyone wanted to do, with the exception of James Brown—somehow his records always rang through. And the Memphis sound was also hard funk.

"We didn't make it on Motown because we basically were like all the other groups, like the Temptations, et cetera. Our problem was that we were too late. From Motown, we went to Golden World, and then Revilot. We had our first big hit on Revilot in 1966, '(I Just Wanna) Testify.' Then we did a few more records and the company folded. That's when we couldn't use the name Parliament anymore. The company was in litigation, and we found out that the name Parliament belonged to them. So it took us three or four years to get the rights to the name back, but in the meantime we became Funkadelic. That was 1968.

"When the name Parliament wasn't usable, I knew we had to have two names from then on. So I signed up Funkadelic as Funkadelic—not George Clinton, not nobody in the group—just Funkadelic. So when we got the name Parliament back, that left us free to sign *them* up to another company. It's only recently that they started using my name. All that ego shit is out to lunch, 'cause it's easy to destroy a name at any time. It's about the group—it ain't about me."

So in their new form, Funkadelic got into a psychedelic funk bag. Drawing on the nastiest, most jagged music around combined with a surrealistic humor and philosophy, they developed a following in the Detroit area, sharing bills with progenitors of new-wave rock like Iggy Pop and the MC5. I told George that to me, his music seemed to synthesize the best elements of people like James Brown, Sly, Hendrix, Sun Ra, Cream, the Art Ensemble of Chicago, the Beatles, Stevie Wonder, Firesign Theatre, Richard Pryor.

"All of the people you've mentioned I've seen at least once or twice. I dig where they are coming from. So they all would have an influence on our approach, either consciously or unconsciously, but definitely the same vibe. Now, I hadn't seen Sun Ra until about a year ago, but I knew it had to be some kind of similarity, because too many people had been making comparisons from 1968 on. When I saw Sun Ra on TV, I dug him. This boy was definitely out there to lunch—the same place I eat at.

"The Sixties was a crazy, cool period. It let us know that we could have an infinite number of alternative realities. Acid busted that shit wide open. But at the time we tried too fast, so we got scared and jumped back. But now that we know what it is, we can sort of sneak up on it slowly."

So in a series of albums on the Westbound label, Funkadelic created their own loose, jamming genre. By 1973 they got back the rights to Parliament, which Clinton signed to Casablanca. Over the course of the next few years, Parliament (representing the arranged), Funkadelic (representing the intuitive), and alumnus Bootsy (representing similar ideas to P-Funk, but aimed at a kiddie audience) developed spectacular stage shows that combined waves of vocals, screaming guitar solos, plain fool humor, and a driving, syncopated pulse with a life philosophy

11

whose purpose is to burn down the ghettos of the mind, tune in to the pure spirit (funk), release inhibitions, get off, and overcome the enervating effects of the *syndrome*.

"Funk ain't nothin' but a hyperventilatin' groovin'. That's all that happens when you hold a single pattern, and suddenly you feel like God. All you done is breathe yourself into hyperventilation, and it feel good. It's like taking acid, or Hare Krishna, or sex, or any other chanting or moving.

"It's that black rhythm of the streets. Right now black is so commercial that anything black will be heard. They'll call it something else, but it's still black. Black is what's happening, so anything black will get a real good eye or a real good ear. So it's time for us to *really* rap now in the language and the rhythm that we rap in—it's all acceptable now. And the rhythm is so hip that it can complement all that intellectual shit that's been going on, which is cool to a point. But first we have to put some rhythm in it, and then later on we can add some metafoolishness, too—like the Chinese and the Indian. I think each of the peoples in the world has got something. White people might have that intellect out there; black people have got that rhythm and instincts. Everybody got somethin'—they probably all into the same place—but no one people has the power to do all that is needed to be done, like lead a planet. I think that when all of that shit just gets together in an orgy, really mingles, you'll find out what are the best possible answers to all of our problems. I mean, that's *my* chess game.

"Now, a lot of cats want to keep you from getting to it, because they think it's better when everybody's the same, and all they got to do is push one button. There is a spirit that cats don't want to recognize: a nature, an intuitive thing, an overriding concept system. No one person can put it together. One cat can't play God with it. It ain't to be owned. It takes all of us working together as one—it's all one. If anyone says they have the only way to it, let the sun stop shining on that motherfucker. Anyone that thinks they are deep enough to be the only one is truly tripping."

Sounds like Zen to me, George.

"Except that we don't teach you what to think, but that you *can* think. Because in this society they teach you that you *can't* think. If you just know that you can, and that it's even okay to think a little *different*, then you cool.

"Now, you can call it what you wanna, and you can sell it to people, because it feels so good. Mutha be ready to buy it—'give me a bag of *that*.' But it's the same shit we all got in us, and motherfuckers been selling *us* for years. And that's what they're doing to us right now. I mean, anybody can be funky.

"And that's why so many people are fucked up in the discos now. They done got to a little dance music, *but that's as far as they can go*. I mean, disco started out as basic R&B, like Motown, but with a nine on it—like a bag of street shit that's been stepped on. There ain't nothin' wrong with it, it's just that they got the same tempo and tones. That's what's dangerous—there isn't a wide enough spectrum. They took a little of the bottom off it, and sweetened it up. It's as if the real low bass tones and the real high frequencies are dirty words on the radio. They don't want you to experience that, 'cause then you want to fuck. All that shit hits you right on your primal notes. They don't want you dabbling in that because you might get some other notions—something bizarre. Notice on radio the records that make it all the way to the top are real light, which is cool, but it's just a step or two above Muzak. They try and compute your every experience, so they'll give you just enough of it for them to tune your tone controls.

"It can get deeper than that. It can get what you call spiritual. It can free your mind so your ass will follow, till you out there acting the fool and *you never thought you could*; out there at a concert waving your hands, shaking your ass, doing the idiot jerk—and really be cool. You know what I'm saying?

"Some people don't want to deal with that. They want somebody to think it all out for them: tell them where it goes, how to get it, and how long to stay. That's why the main thing in the world today is 'I can't come.' Because people have no real control over their sensitivity or their communication. I mean, you can get ready to get some and you won't get up, because the last time you tried to get some, it was toothpaste. You get orchestrated toward that, and your body adrenaline gets ready for sex because of a commercial; then when you call for your body to do something for you, it can't, because you done overrode it all day watching TV—until you have no sensitivity of the real thing. So your body says, 'Screw you, man, you told me that was the real thing this afternoon and it wasn't nothing but Crest.'

"I call all of that shit *tempo tampering*. You're trying to dance, and somebody puts their finger on the record. They override your primal things with interference, and make you think the way they want you to. It's called *subliminal*, but man, it works like a motherfucker."

All of this is starting to sound like *1984*.

"Sheeet, they way past that now. You have to think the next war will be a mental one; there's no percentage in physical war. Believe me, those behaviorist motherfuckers are bad, Jack. They didn't go to school and french with that trash just to make rats walk a figure eight. They can program your ass. All of this tempo tampering is what's making cats go out. They got us going in both directions at once. They tell you not to get it; not to mingle with it and get wild and play; because that's obscene, it's immoral. But then all of the commercials in the world are based on sex— everything is based on sex—and you desire and lust and they call your feelings a sin. Some cats go crazy. They are playing with the forms and interpretations all the time. As long as they can label the interpretations, sell them back to you, and tell you what is or isn't logical, they can make you crazy. They planned that one up because they can't burn the witches no more, so they just changed the concept. Now they call you crazy. Insane is the new hell, 'cause if God is dead, then that means the Devil's out of a gig, too. But people will still react to some poor motherfucker going nuts. We got a street expression called a dooloop where you give a thing a new meaning; turn it upside down, change the underlying concept. Take the word *cult*. They done doolooped that so that the word is out for a minute, because they make you think that when you mess with them forces, you get out of control. So leave the driving to us, those forces not to be messed with, trust us. The system is the solution. Don't do nothing crazy. But deep down, we know they is full of shit—that *crazy is cool*.

"So at certain times you have to change the words you use to describe something. Change the interpretation of something, even though the *essence* is still the same. Like the word *funk*—we can use the word as long as we need to use the word. But if it came to a matter of survival where we were identified with the word, then we could just change it. But the rhythms would always go on being the same. Because funk by any other name would still be funky—still make a motherfucker say shit, it damn near smell. 'Cause it's that primal thing, and that funny kind of nasty humor. Cats can't be cool when they hear that music. And you either love it 'cause it will make you twitch, or you hate it. But if you stay with it, *you will dance*."

We must now take leave of Dr. Funkenstein. You may wonder why the pastor of such an unsanctified church is allowed on the loose. "When you are making *them* money," Clinton says, "you no longer crazy—you just *eccentric*. But if you just some poor street nigger, then you plain *crazy*."

Dr. Funkenstein may be crazy, but he is not insane. He has, in effect, got four or five different record companies putting out albums by the *same* basic group, so that all of them have an interest in promoting whoever is on tour. He gives twenty-five cents of every ticket sold at the Parliaments/Funkadelic concerts to the United Negro College Fund. He comes up with so many new slants on the same stroke that his fans have come to expect—no, demand—surprises. And he even manages to laugh at the terrifying Orwellian world he prophesies—divine stupidity, he calls it.

"You can have a lot of choices of what to do with our music. You can dance to it or listen to it, but you don't have to get real serious with it. It can just be funny. 'Cause to me it's just funny that it can be all of these different things, and we don't have to feel seriously life and death about any portion of it."

April 1979

PAUL MCCARTNEY:
LIFTING THE VEIL ON
THE BEATLES

BY VIC GARBARINI

I'm sitting in a large,

sparsely furnished apartment somewhere in north

London. Paul McCartney is seated across from me,

patiently sipping a cup of tea as he waits for me to

set up my tape recorder. Finally, I'm ready to go. I'm

just launching into my first question when McCart-

ney suddenly turns toward the door and smiles. I

watch in amazement as both John Lennon and

George Harrison enter the room. "Ringo couldn't

make it," says McCartney, still smiling. I open my

mouth to answer him, but instead of words, only a ringing bell-like noise comes out. . . .

Woke up, fell out of bed, Dragged a comb across my head. Shit. Shit. It's 8:20 already. I wearily grope for the clock, making a mental note to ask my dad to fix the alarm. As I stagger into the bathroom I remember about the geometry test. *The geometry test!* I'd forgotten all about it! Two minutes of pure panic ensue as I feverishly search my memory: *relief.* I sit behind Mraz in Geometry. The math freak. The guy I loaned last month's copy of *Playboy* to. *Good ol' Mraz . . . Found my coat and grabbed my hat, Made the bus in seconds flat. Found my way upstairs and had a smoke, Somebody spoke and I went into a dream. . . .*

"Sugar?"

"Huh?"

"Sugar," repeats Paul McCartney. "Do you want sugar in your tea?"

"Uh, right. Sorry. Drifted off there for a minute." Be cool, thinks I. Engage the critical faculties. He's just another bloke. Wrote a lot of good songs. *Transformed my generation.* Hasn't done much interesting lately. Sure, he's talented and his music changed my life. But he's only human. *So why do I feel like I'm having a conversation with my own childhood?* Hold on now. Let's get some perspective here: Carl Jung actually had conversations with his archetypes. *Yeah,* responds a tiny voice, *but did one of them ever put sugar in his tea?* Point taken. *When I get older, losing my hair, Many years from now . . .*

Natural. Unpretentious. Those are the words that best describe James Paul McCartney at thirty-eight, ten years after the breakup of the most influential pop group the world has ever known. The boyish good looks are still remarkably intact (no hair loss, though most of the baby fat is gone), but what impresses most is his relaxed, open manner. He seemed totally at ease during our two-hour conversation at his London offices. He was charming, frank, and surprisingly willing to talk at great length about the Beatles experience. *Willing* isn't the right word—he seemed positively *eager* to discuss it, for reasons he explains fully in the interview. Paul claims he wants to be just an ordinary guy, and I believe him. He's anchored himself in normalcy, reasonably secure in the nest he's created with his family and farm. As a result, his work with Wings has sometimes lacked creative tension—a problem which many critics, myself included, find irksome. Great art often requires friction—something to struggle against, an inner or outer obstacle to overcome in order to get the creative juices flowing and provide energy. Externally, there's little for McCartney to rub up against these days, and he doesn't seem to harbor the kind of inner demons that can drive John Lennon to tantrums and transcendence. But when he's offered a challenge, as in the case of the nearly disastrous *Band on the Run* sessions—or in a concert situation, as captured on the excellent *Wings Over America* live set—McCartney has proven that he can still turn out material that rivals his work with the Beatles. His creative potential may be underutilized at times, but his powers seem relatively undiminished. In fact, his new solo album, *McCartney II*, contains some of his best material since *Abbey Road*. True, there's relatively little tension here, but in this case it hardly seems to matter: This is pure, distilled, essence of McCartney—gorgeous, dreamlike melodies floating through Eno-esque electronic textures, ranging from the Bach-like elegance and soothing ethereality of "Summer Day Song" to the poignant romanticism of "Waterfalls." His work may occasionally disappoint, but I'm heartened that a man who's been through what McCartney has can remain so open and unspoiled and still capable of creative work of this caliber.

They've been going in and out of style
But they're guaranteed to raise a smile
So may I introduce to you
The act you've known for all these years . . .

MUSICIAN: *Let's just skip over the whole Japan thing. I'm
sure you're sick of answering questions about it by now.
Needless to say, you won't have a* Live at Budokan *album
coming out this year.*

McCARTNEY: [deadpan] Good joke.

MUSICIAN: *Thanks. I've been saving that one for weeks.
Moving right along: Why another solo album now?*

McCARTNEY: Well, actually I was trying *not* to do an album. It was just after *Back to the Egg*, and I wanted to
do something totally different. So I just plugged a single
microphone into the back of a Studer 16-track tape machine; didn't use a recording console at all. The idea was
that at the end of it I'd just have a zany little cassette that
I'd play in my car and never release. In the end I had a few
tracks, played them for a couple of people, and they said,
"I see, that's your next album." And I thought, "Right, it
probably is." So then I got a bit serious about it and tried
to make it into an "album." That was the worst part of it—
I was having fun till then.

MUSICIAN: *It's interesting the way you describe your approach. It reminds me of the way Eno goes about making
an album—creative play. The other person who came to
mind when I first heard it was Stevie Wonder. . . .*

McCARTNEY: I like Stevie a lot. It's probably because he's
the only other person who's done this kind of recording . . .
doing it all yourself.

MUSICIAN: *You're also the only two people who've combined avant garde electronic textures with an unerring sense
of melody.*

McCARTNEY: Well, I can't help that. I'm glad I can't help

22

that. When I was doing this album I thought I'd make something that didn't sound anything like me. The first three tracks I made were the two instrumentals on the album and a third one which I later put lyrics on. I wanted something that sounded nothing like me, but inevitably you start to creep through even that, your sense of tune or whatever it is.

MUSICIAN: *Have you ever consciously tried to do a melody that was non-diatonic, not based on a major or minor motif or something?*

McCARTNEY: Well, I don't understand that in music. I'm not a technical musician.

MUSICIAN: *Something discordant, something that isn't normal tonal melody.*

McCARTNEY: Yes, on some of the tracks. I had enough for a double album and most of the tracks that came off to make a single album were a bit more like that. One was kind of sequences of wobble noises, a crazy track, probably not worth releasing, it's just for the cassette in my car. There are people who like it but it's just experimental. I like it, but . . . zoning in on which ones we were going to release, I asked a lot of people which were their favorites, and the ones that got dropped off were probably the least me. I've got one ten-minute instrumental that just goes on forever and forever.

MUSICIAN: *And you left off the ones that were less melodic. Could you ever conceive of putting out the experimental stuff?*

McCARTNEY: I wouldn't mind it. The thing is, I go through record companies and record companies want to have a say in it. If I bring them an album that they think is totally uncommercial, and I say, "Look, artistically I've got to do this . . ." you have to agree with them in the end when they say, "Look, it's very nice but we'd rather have this please because we're the company that's going to release it." I'm not going in an avant garde direction particularly—it's just for my own interest, that sort of stuff—but still I get certain decisions creeping in that wouldn't necessarily be my decisions.

MUSICIAN: *You're forgiven. Were you very disappointed or surprised by the negative critical reaction to* Back to the Egg?

McCARTNEY: I'm used to all that now. Nearly everything I've ever done or been involved in has received some negative critical reaction. You'd think the response to something like "She Loves You" with the Beatles would have been pretty positive. It wasn't. The very first week that came out it was supposed to be the *worst* song the Beatles had ever thought of doing. Then *Ram* was supposed to be the *worst* thing I'd ever done. And so the criticism continues.

MUSICIAN: *But was the harder rocking approach on* Back to the Egg *a reaction to criticism of your work as too poppish? Were you influenced by the emergence of New Wave?*

McCARTNEY: It was just what I was into at the time. The New Wave thing was happening, and I realized that a lot of New Wave was just taking things at a faster tempo than we do—"we" being what I like to call the *Permanent Wave* (little joke there ...). So you get something like "Spin It Out" out of that. I'm always getting influence. Most of the songs I've written can be traced to some kind of influence—Elvis Presley, Carl Perkins, Chuck Berry to name a few. Even some of the Thirties-type tunes like "When I'm Sixty-four" or "Honey Pie." That's influenced by Fred Astaire and people like that.

MUSICIAN: *Can you look at your own work with any degree of objectivity or impartiality? I mean, can you listen to an album you've just made and trust yourself to be able to see what its strong and weak points are?*

McCARTNEY: When they first come out, I'm totally confused. It takes a few months for me to warm up to them. Sometimes I'll be at a party, and I'll hear music coming from the next room. Immediately I'll get jealous and think "Who's that?" So I go into the other room and it's *us*. And I think, "Hey, I *like* this group—we're all right after all!" Because everyone's a bit paranoid.

MUSICIAN: Band on the Run *was probably the most successful Wings album from both a commercial and critical standpoint. Was it the most satisfying one for you?*

McCARTNEY: I like *Band on the Run*. That was going to be a normal Wings album originally, but then our guitarist at the time, Henry McCullough, and Denny Seiwell failed to turn up. It was one of those numbers where they said, "We don't want to go to Lagos and record this album, sorry." I was left in the lurch at the last minute—literally an hour before the flight. So there was just Denny Laine, Linda, and myself in Nigeria. I played drums, bass, and a lot of guitar myself—I took a lot of control on that album. It was almost a solo album.

MUSICIAN: *Why Lagos?*

McCARTNEY: I just fancied going to Africa; I'm into African rhythms. While we were there I saw the best band I've ever seen live. Fela Ramsomekuty, it was. I think he's in jail now; he's too political for the local authorities. We saw him one night at his own club and I was *crying*. A lot of it was just relief. There were a lot of crazy circumstances and weird things happening. At one point we got held up at knifepoint. It was a real fight to make that album.

MUSICIAN: *Do you find in your experience that friction like that can actually help the creative process?*

McCARTNEY: Unfortunately, yes, it does help. It's unfortunate because who wants to go around having stress all the time just to aid creativity? But when it happens it does actually seem to help. It's a drag because the logic then follows is that we should all walk around even more stressed to make better albums. Who needs it? I'd rather not make albums than do that. But it did help on *Band on the Run*; it gave us something to fight against. At first I was worried. But then I thought, "Wait a minute, I love playing drums." So the positive side started to creep in, too.

MUSICIAN: *I've heard that with the Beatles you sometimes gave Ringo directions regarding what he should play.*

McCARTNEY: We *always* gave Ringo direction—on every single number. It was usually very controlled. Whoever had written the song—John, for instance—would say, "I want this." Obviously a lot of the stuff came out of what Ringo was playing; but we would always control it.

MUSICIAN: *Did musical disagreements or conflicts have anything to do with the breakup?*

McCARTNEY: They were some of the minor reasons, yeah. I remember on "Hey Jude," telling George not to play guitar. He wanted to echo riffs after the vocal phrases, which I didn't think was appropriate. He didn't see it like that, and it was a bit of a number for me to have to *dare* to tell George Harrison—who's one of the greats, I think— not to play. It was like an insult. But that was how we did a lot of our stuff.

MUSICIAN: *We were talking about creative tension, and how even if it's a pain in the ass it can be useful. Are there any particular Beatle albums that—*

MUSICIAN: The *White Album*. That was the tension album. We were all in the midst of the psychedelic thing, or just coming out of it. In any case, it was weird. Never before had we recorded with beds in the studio and people visiting for hours on end; business meetings and all that. There was a lot of friction during that album.

MUSICIAN: *That was the one that sounded the most fragmented to me, whereas* Abbey Road *sounded the smoothest. Yet I imagine there was a lot of tension at that point, too.*

McCARTNEY: No, not really, there was ... no, come to

think of it, there *was* actually, yes. There were one or two tense moments. But it didn't feel like a tense album to me; I was busy getting into a lot of new musical ideas, like the medley thing on the second side. I think the *White Album* was the weirdest experience because we were about to break up. And that was just tense in itself.

MUSICIAN: *I want to ask you about your bass playing. To me you've always played bass like a frustrated guitar player. Those melodic lines that started to show up on* Sgt. Pepper— *there was no precedent for that in rock music. How did that style of playing come about?*

MCCARTNEY: I'd always liked those little lines that worked as support, and yet had their own identity instead of just staying in the background. Also, bass was beginning to come to the fore in mixes at that point. If you listen to early Beatle mixes, the bass and bass drum aren't there. We were starting to take over mixing ourselves, and to bring those things out, so I had to do something with it. I was listening to a lot of Motown and Stax at the time, Marvin Gaye and people like that.

MUSICIAN: *How did* Sgt. Pepper *come about?*

MCCARTNEY: I think the big influence was *Pet Sounds* by the Beach Boys. That album just flipped me. Still is one of my favorite albums—the musical invention on that is just amazing. I play it for our kids now and they love it. When I heard it I thought, "Oh dear, this is the album of all time. What the hell are we going to do?" My ideas took off from that standard.

MUSICIAN: *Wasn't the initial concept some kind of fantasy thing?*

MCCARTNEY: Yeah, I had this idea that it was going to be an album of another band that wasn't us—we'd just imagine all the time that it wasn't us playing. It was just a nice little device to give us some distance on the album.

MUSICIAN: *I remember listening to it and thinking it was*

the perfect fantasy album; you could put yourself into a whole other world. That's really the way you went about creating it, then.

McCARTNEY: Right. That was the whole idea. The cover was going to be us dressed as this other band in crazy gear; but it was all stuff that we'd always wanted to wear. And we were going to have photos on the wall of all our heroes: Marlon Brando in his leather jacket, Einstein—it could be anybody who we'd ever thought was good. Cult heroes. And we kind of put this other identity on them to do it. It changed a lot in the process, but that was the basic idea behind it.

MUSICIAN: *Thinking back on that period, which album would you say caught the feeling of expansion and creativity that was going on at its height?*

McCARTNEY: *Pepper* probably. . . .

MUSICIAN: *What about* Rubber Soul? *That was a real departure. . . .*

McCARTNEY: All I can remember is that it was a kind of straightforward album . . .

MUSICIAN: *It was so acoustic, though, compared to the previous stuff.*

McCARTNEY: Those were the sounds we were into at the time. "You've Got to Hide Your Love Away" is just basically John doing Dylan. Dylan had just come out and we were big fans of his. *Rubber Soul* was just a catchy title; that's the bit I remember most about it. A lot of people liked that as an album.

MUSICIAN: *Among connoisseurs it's considered one of the early high points.* Revolver *too. . . .*

McCARTNEY: Just to show you how wrong one can be: I was in Germany on tour just before *Revolver* came out. I started listening to the album and I got really down because *I thought the whole thing was out of tune.* Everyone had to reassure me that it was okay.

MUSICIAN: *Robert Fripp wrote a piece for us recently in which he talked about an artist's image, and how it can have a life of its own. In the sense that you're Paul McCartney, a human being with tastes, talents, faults, and all that; and yet you also have a public image—as Johnny Lydon would say—that has a life of its own that's almost independent of you. Sometimes people relate to that image instead of to you as a person. How did you deal with this when you first encountered it with the Beatles? Did it bother you? Was it enjoyable? How did it feel from the inside?*

McCARTNEY: At first you're just an ordinary Joe rockin' around trying to make a living. Then you get famous; you get your first hit and you love it. There's nothing you'd like to do more than sign autographs: *You got 'em—I'll do 'em.* That wears off after three or four years. You start to think, "Wait a minute, what am I bloody signing for you for?" At this point I've come to another phase where I think it's all okay again. So I've been in and out of that.

MUSICIAN: *Have you ever wished you could just chuck it all and fade into obscurity?*

McCARTNEY: I remember thinking at one point that I've come to a point of no return; that even if I say now that I don't want to be famous anymore, I'll be like Brigitte Bardot or Charlie Chaplin: a recluse but still very famous. And that's no use—they'll be after me even more.

MUSICIAN: *Do you think that was John's reaction?*

McCARTNEY: I really don't like to speak for John. But seeing as how you've asked me, my theory is that he's done all the things he wants to do except one—being himself. Now he's just turned on to actually living his own life—sod everyone else. But it's not an aggressive thing, from what I can see.

MUSICIAN: *Muscially you're the most active of the former Beatles. You maintain a band and still tour pretty consistently, which the others don't. I don't want to get into a comparison trip, but after being with the Beatles, where do you go?*

McCARTNEY: It's rather difficult to top, yeah.

MUSICIAN: *All of you must have felt some trepidation at the thought of going out on your own, but you didn't seem to worry. . . .*

McCARTNEY: I didn't *seem* to, but that's one of my features: I may seem to not do a lot of things, when in fact I can be just as bad as the next guy. The first gigs we did with Wings were frightening; it was so scary coming out with a new band knowing the Beatles was what was expected. But it was just a question of knowing I had to run that gauntlet, go through that thing, and that once I came out of it, I'd feel better and be glad I'd gone through it.

MUSICIAN: *Did you ever experience that kind of fear with the Beatles?*

McCARTNEY: Sure. I remember many times just sitting outside concert halls waiting for the police to escort us inside and thinking, "Jesus Christ, I really don't want to go through this. We've done enough, let's take the money and run! Let's go down to Brighton, or something." Linda and I felt like that when she was having our last baby. We were driving to the hospital and there was this terrible desire to say, "Let's go to Brighton instead." If we could have gotten away with it, we would have.

MUSICIAN: *Those early tours with Wings were pretty innovative for the time: showing up unannounced at colleges in a van and charging only a dollar admission. Exactly the kind of impromptu "small is beautiful" philosophy that a lot of the New Wavers are beginning to espouse, only you were doing it eight years ago. What led you to take that approach?*

McCARTNEY: Instead of doing what was expected, I asked myself, "What do I *really* want to do?" What have I missed being with the Beatles? What is it time to do? It was silly little things, like with the Beatles you used to get paid massively, but you never saw it because it always went straight into the company. You had to draw on it. So for me one of the buzzes of that first tour was actually getting a bag of coins at the end of the gig. It wasn't just a materialistic thing—it was the feeling of getting physically paid again; it was like going back to square one. I wanted to take it back to where the Beatles started, which was in the halls. We charged 50p to get in—obviously we could have charged more—and gave the Student Union a bit for having us there. We played poker with the money afterwards, and I'd actually pay the band physically, you know, *"50p for you . . . and 50p for you."* It brought back the thrill of actually working for a living.

MUSICIAN: *Can you empathize with this New Wave thing? Did you feel that same explosive force with the early Beatles in Hamburg and elsewhere?*

MCCARTNEY: Yes, I think it's the same thing, and will always be the same. It's just a question of age: When we were eighteen, we were doing it and getting exactly the same reaction, only twenty years earlier. It's the energy. I don't care where they got it from, if it sounds like a great piece of music—the Sex Pistols' "Pretty Vacant," for instance—then I'm all for it.

MUSICIAN: *Some of the early Beatle material was obviously coming out of Chuck Berry and Buddy Holly, but most of it seemed strikingly original. How did that Merseybeat sound come about?*

MCCARTNEY: When we started the Beatles, John and I sat down and wrote about fifty songs, out of which I think "Love Me Do" is the only one that got published. Those songs weren't very good because we were trying to find the next beat—*the next new sound. New Musical Express*—which was a much gentler paper at the time—was talking about calypso, and how Latin rock was going to be the next big thing. The minute we stopped trying to *find* that new beat, the newspapers started saying it was *us*; and we found we'd discovered the new sound without even trying. That's what made me suspicious of categories like heavy metal or pop. My musical tastes range from Fred Astaire to the Sex Pistols and everything in between: Pink Floyd, Stevie Wonder, the Stones. . . .

MUSICIAN: *A great deal of the criticism you've come in for seems to be because you use pop as a medium. What is it about pop you're attracted to?*

McCARTNEY: I just like it. I'm like a lot of people—when I get in my car and turn on the radio, I want to hear some good sounds. So whatever I write, I write for that. What are the alternatives? To write a "serious" piece of music. Or modern classical music? No thanks. I'd bore myself stiff after a couple of bars.

MUSICIAN: *The first major cultural experience of my generation was in February 1964 when we saw you on "The Ed Sullivan Show." It was like something just swept over the whole country, a new, open energy. . . .*

McCARTNEY: It was strange, wasn't it?

MUSICIAN: *What the hell was it all about?*

McCARTNEY: I don't know. I personally think that in America there was a standard way of doing things. The only freaky people were Hollywood writers, jazz musicians, and pop stars, but even they were tied to a framework. Meanwhile we had cooked up this whole new British thing; we had a long time to work it out and make all our mistakes in Hamburg with almost no one watching. We were very different, having taken all the American influences and stewed them up in a British way. A lot of things had been happening with our own chemistry, 'cause John and I were strong writers, George was like a third writer, Ringo who had a good head on his shoulders and was by no means thick . . . We'd put in a lot of work. In Hamburg we'd work eight hours a day; most bands never worked that hard. We literally worked eight hours a day, it was a full factory day. So we had developed our act by the time we came to America we had worked all that out. All the success we'd had in Britain—the British newspapers were saying, well, what's left to do, you've conquered everything, and we'd say, AMERICA. We got the Number One, did "Ed Sullivan" . . . by then we'd distilled our stuff down to an essence, so we weren't just coming on as any old band. We had our own totally new identities. . . .

MUSICIAN: *Did you feel that among you, was—*

McCARTNEY: Yes, we knew it. People were saying, "What's this with the haircut?" If I go back on the haircut thing, I know it was actually because we saw some guy in Hamburg whose hair we liked. John and I were hitching to Paris and we asked him to cut our hair like he did his; he didn't do it quite the same and it fell down in a Beatles cut. He was a very sort of artsy guy this guy, great guy called Jurgen. He cut our hair, we came back to England. All the people in England thought we were German, 'cause the newspapers said, "Direct from Hamburg." All the kids were surprised when they saw us. We had leather jackets and blue jeans. We thought we won't have corny suits, we'll have new things, Cardin jackets. So by the time we got to the States, for instance . . . the hair, which was really a bit of an accident, and was really what a lot of artsy people were doing anyway, we were the first with it in the States, so it looked like we'd invented it. Actually the story was a lot more ordinary. Like life is. But by the time it got to be presented on "The Ed Sullivan Show," the biggest show in the States, and there we were with these funny haircuts, it was us. Everybody said, "You started the Beatle haircut." So it was like distilling the essence of what we were going through and laying it all on America in one big move. That's why it was such a big shock and had such a big effect on them.

MUSICIAN: *Was it apparent to you that something was going on that was more than just another very big group—that this was a cultural phenomenon?*

McCARTNEY: You don't get into that. I don't think that when Muhammad Ali was shouting he was the greatest that he actually *knew* he was—it was bluff. Show biz. He *suspected* he was; we suspected we were. But a lot of what you did was just bluff, because if you want to be Number One, you *tell* everyone you're number one.

MUSICIAN: *But when did you realize "My God, it worked!"? This is more than just a musical event; this is a whole generation. . . .*

McCARTNEY: Very early on. When we started off in Hamburg we had no audience, so we had to work our asses off to get people in. People would appear at the door of the club while we were onstage, and there would be nobody at the tables. We used to try to get them in to sell beer. The minute we saw someone we'd kick into "Dancing in the Streets"—which was one of our big numbers at the time—and just rock out, pretending we hadn't seen them. And we'd find we'd got three of them in. We were like fairground barkers: *see four people—have to get them in.* We eventually sold the club out, which is when we realized it was going to get really big. Then we went back to England and played the Cavern; same thing happened there. First nobody came; then they started coming in; finally they came in droves. There was this incredible excitement. So we knew something we were doing must have been right. By the time we started playing tours it really didn't surprise us anymore, though we were still thrilled by it all. When we were on the Chris Montez tour, he was on the top of the bill; halfway through they switched it and put us on top. It was embarassing as hell for him—I mean, what could you say to him? Sorry, Chris? He took it well and stuff, but we expected it by then. Everywhere we'd gone it'd seemed to work.

MUSICIAN: *At that point no European group had ever really conquered America—no pop group. How did you determine when you were ready to take the plunge and come to the U.S.?*

McCARTNEY: The thing we did—which I always think new groups should take as a bit of advice—was that we were cheeky enough to say that we wouldn't go to the States until we had a Number One record there. We were offered tours, but we knew we'd be second to someone and we didn't want that. There was a lot of careful thought behind it. There were a lot of artists from here who'd go over and vanish. Cliff Richard's still trying to make it in the States. We always looked at it logically and thought, "Well, that's the mistake. You've got to go in as Number One." So there was a lot of careful thought there, we were cooking up this act, the Beatles. It was very European, very British as opposed to the standard American way of doing things: Ed, couple of jugglers, Sinatra, Sinatra Jr., even Elvis from the waist up. The American Dream.

MUSICIAN: *Can you remember what it was like when it finally happened?*

McCARTNEY: When we heard that our first record went Number One in the States? Yeah. We were playing Paris at the time. The telegram came and we all jumped on each other's backs and ran around everywhere. Big Mal the roadie gave everyone piggyback rides—we were just so excited. So we went to America, and it was all like we'd planned might happen. But we were lucky; it went much further than we'd ever imagined.

MUSICIAN: *What was it that made the group able to weather the incredible pressure of all that and stay together as long as it did?*

McCARTNEY: It didn't feel like pressure—it wasn't pressure for a long time. At American press conferences, they used to ask, "What will you do when the bubble bursts?" There used to be a guy like yourself who we'd take around with us 'cause he was so funny. We used to ask him to ask that question every time—it was the only question he ever asked on the whole tour. He got to be like a court jester.

MUSICIAN: *So how did you answer him?*

McCARTNEY: I don't know—we'll blow up or we'll fall out of the sky or whatever. . . . But it was never a serious question to us.

MUSICIAN: *When and why did the bubble burst?*

McCARTNEY: I don't know, really. Just about a year before the Beatles broke up. You could say the seed was sown from very early on. I don't know—it just did. Friction came in; business things; relations between us. We were all looking for people in our lives. John had found Yoko; it made things very difficult. He wanted a very intense, intimate life with her; at the same time we'd always reserved that kind of intimacy for the group. You could understand that he had to have time with her. But does he have to have *that* much time with her was sort of the feeling of the group. So these things just started to create immovable objects and pressures that were just too big. After that—after the breakup—then the idea of when-will-the-bubble-burst came home. So I thought, "Oh, *that* was what that guy was talking about at every bloody press conference!" We weren't aware of that much pressure while the Beatles were happening because we were a very organized group—a well-rehearsed unit. But eventually I started to realize what they were talking about. When you start to grow up you realize, "Wait a minute, I really am holding down a job here and if my paid gig goes down. . . ."

MUSICIAN: *I'm impressed by how easily you can go back into that period and pull out all these things. I was afraid you might not be willing to talk about the Beatles; it seemed like a forbidden topic for so long. . . .*

McCARTNEY: Well, I recently did this video clip on which I play all the instruments like I do on the album. We had to think of someone to make the bass player like. So I told the director I could do Beatle Paul. And he said, "Yeah, you've gotta do it." I almost chickened out in the end. But I did it and put on my old uniform and got out the old Hofner Violin bass—which still has a song list from the Beatles taped to it—and I didn't realize till a few days later that I'd gone and broken the whole voodoo of talking about the Beatles. . . . 'Cause I'd been him again and it didn't feel bad. I mean if someone else is going to impersonate me, I might as well do it myself. And it was such a ball among the studio technicians—they really got off on it.

MUSICIAN: *Did it feel like you were stepping back into that old image for a minute?*

McCARTNEY: Yes. I felt great. It felt like I was on a TV show twenty years ago—exactly the same. The bass was the same weight—the whole thing about the Hofner bass is that it's like balsa wood. It's so comfortable after a Fender or a Rickenbacker. I now play a Rickenbacker or a Yamaha, which are quite heavy.

MUSICIAN: *Why did you switch?*

McCARTNEY: It was given to me. Back in the mid-Sixties Mr. Rickenbacker gave me a special left-handed bass. It was the first left-handed bass I'd ever had, 'cause the Hofner was a converted right hand. It was a freebie and I loved it; I started getting into it on *Sgt. Pepper.* And now I'm playing a Yamaha.

MUSICIAN: *How come?*

MCCARTNEY: Because they gave me one—I'm anybody's for a free guitar! Sometimes I think I should research what instrument I like to play best. But generally I seem to play stuff that's been given me. Naturally I only play the stuff that I like—I've been given stuff that I don't care for—but I like it like that. I don't like things to be too thought out and logical. If someone asked me what strings I used, I honestly couldn't tell them—they come out of a little bag. To me these things are just vehicles. They're beautiful and I love them, but I don't want to find out too much about them. It's just the way my mind is; I'd prefer to be non-technical.

MUSICIAN: *What about your composing and writing? Do you have a set way of going about putting together a song, or is it all pretty free-flowing?*

MCCARTNEY: I'm suspicious of formulas: The minute I've got a formula, I try and change it. People used to ask us what comes first, the music or the words? Or Lennon and McCartney, who does what? We all did a bit of everything. Sometimes I wrote the words and sometimes John did; sometimes I'd write a tune and sometimes he would.

MUSICIAN: . . . were *you the Walrus?*

MCCARTNEY: Yeah. I'm *still* the Walrus. That was a nothing thing, really, didn't mean anything. What happened was that during *Magical Mystery Tour* we did a scene where we all put on masks—it happens to be me with the Walrus mask. We just picked up a head each; no thought behind it. Then there was all that stuff about me being dead. . . .

MUSICIAN: *I think it's amazing that your bass playing continued to improve after you died. Very impressive.*

MCCARTNEY: Hmmm . . . yes. Then there was that whole thing about me wearing a black carnation. I had a black carnation because they'd run out of red ones. So there was this *hugely* significant thing of me wearing a black carnation. Or turning my back on the *Sgt. Pepper* cover—it was actually just a goof. When we were doing the photos I turned my back . . . it was like a joke or whatever.

MUSICIAN: *Are your good feelings about New Wave because you recognize the same kind of creative element you cultivated with the Beatles?*

MCCARTNEY: I think the nice thing about New Wave is that it's gotten back to real music, rather than pop. I don't like a lot of it . . . a lot of it I do like. I can see where it's all come from. A great deal of it you can trace back to the Doors, Lou Reed, Bowie, and Brian Ferry. But that's great. I was influenced by Elvis; I still do an Elvis impersonation at a party, "Love Me Tender." I recognize that we're all these very frail . . . no matter who puts on the great show out front, basically we are all imitators. We used to nick songs, titles, John and I. I've even been inspired by things in the press. "Helter Skelter" came about because I read in *Melody Maker* that the Who had made some track or other that was the loudest, most raucous rock 'n' roll, the dirtiest thing they'd ever done. I didn't know what track they were talking about but it made me think, "Right. Got to do it." And I totally got off on that one little sentence in the paper, and I said, "We've got to do the loudest, most raucous . . ." And that ended up as "Helter Skelter." But that's great. We were the greatest criminals going.

MUSICIAN: *Getting back to your own writing, I've noticed that with Wings your writing often centers on themes having to do with the home, domesticity, and the family. Is that a reaction to the craziness of the Beatles and the Sixties in general?*

MCCARTNEY: It came out of getting married. Everything changes in the way you look at things. I started realizing that I liked the warmth of a family—the no-hassle thing of having a family you can relate to intimately without really trying. When you're eighteen you sneer at all that kind of thing. But when you're thirty you start to reconsider: *What do I really think about all that?* When my dad used to hit me as a kid, he'd say, "When you've got kids of your own, you'll understand." And I thought, "You're a lunatic! You're hitting me and I'll *never* understand that." Then you get a few kids and you realize what he was talking about. Only time can do that. The word *home* changed its meaning after I'd gotten married. I'd never really had a home for a long time. I started to realize that it's important to investigate your feelings instead of hiding them.

MUSICIAN: *Looking back over your career, do you feel satisfied? Do you feel content when you consider your musical legacy?*

MCCARTNEY: I'd say I've done some songs that I think are really good; some that I think didn't quite come off; some I hate. But I've done enough to satisfy myself that I'm okay. That's basically all I'm looking for. Like most people.

MUSICIAN: *As long as you stay in touch with your own creativity, as you said, and keep going through this reviving, refreshing process.*

MCCARTNEY: Yes, as long as there's still some good music coming out. There'll be a wave of bad music out there and then something'll come along and kick it. They may be swearing and picking their noses and cutting themselves, but if they bring out good . . . if the energy is there regardless of the form . . . if it's Merseybeat or Potatobeat it makes no difference to me, as long as there's something there. There's a great trick about records, it has to leap off the plastic and if it does, it's magic. How is it that some leap off the plastic and some don't? I don't care who does it, or how. It can be Segovia or Johnny Rotten, as long as they're communicating.

MUSICIAN: *To me, the deepest song you've done since the*

Beatles is "One of These Days" on the new album. What's going to happen one of these days?

MCCARTNEY: But doesn't everyone have this kind of thing in them, since they're a kid, that one of these days I'll get round to it? I've always wanted to be a friendly person; well, one of these days I'm going to *be* a friendly person. But in the meantime life gets in the way and you don't always find yourself being friendly.... It's just groping in the dark really, but a lot of what I do is like that, and I don't see any alternative to it. But I think of that as a positive thing. I don't know what I was before I was born. I was the sperm that won out of those three hundred million. I can't remember that far back, but there was something working for me, some incredible thing that did it. So for me the wonder of that, of knowing that something got on with it before my conscious memory existed, leads me to believe that when you die maybe something gets on with it, too. Which gives me this vague faith that I can't pinpoint. I don't say it's so-and-so doing it. But it's just IT, and whatever IT is, I have an optimistic view about it. Based on the record that it got me this far, it can't be *that* bad, right?

August 1980

BRUCE SPRINGSTEEN

HAS NO PRICE

BY DAVE MARSH

■

A *year ago, taking a respite*

from recording to play two nights of the M.U.S.E. anti-

nuke concerts, Bruce Springsteen pared his normal

three-hour show down to a more everyday ninety

minutes. The result was pandemonium just this side of

Beatlemania. Following the biggest stars in American

soft rock to the Madison Square Garden stage,

Springsteen and the E Street Band upstaged everyone,

including the issue itself. The air in the hall that night

was one of fanaticism and conversion, as though

Springsteen were a rock 'n' roll evangelist and the Garden his tabernacle.

It's easy to imagine that Springsteen was just a pro rising to an occasion which included a camera crew and a recording truck, not to mention a backstage full of peers. What's harder to explain, unless you've seen him onstage before a crowd that might not include so much as a weekly newspaper reviewer, is that the M.U.S.E. shows were just a fragment of what he usually does. "After those shows went over so great, I just figured that that's what we'd be doing on this tour," remembers E Street guitarist Steve Van Zandt. "Just ninety minutes, a couple of ballads, and make people as crazy as you can, like the old days. We can do that, but not Bruce. What we ended up doing was just adding that ninety minutes to the show we always did."

By late October, when the E Streeters hit L.A. for four shows at the fifteen-thousand-seat Sports Arena, they were playing four-and-one-half-hour shows five nights a week. Going on at eight-thirty, they'd break at ten and return a half hour later to play until a quarter to one—or one or one-fifteen. And they weren't playing the ebb-and-flow show offered by most bands who play so long. We're talking about four hours of ensemble rock 'n' roll here, in which even the ballads are attacked more strenuously than most modal jams. Yet Springsteen's manager Jon Landau said one night, "I think Bruce might actually play longer, except that the band just gets worn out." True enough, drummer Max Weinberg often spends intermission taping bleeding fingers, and the others are spared such medicaments only because their instruments are less physically demanding.

Generally, Springsteen did thirty-two or thirty-three songs, including seventeen or eighteen from *The River*, a half dozen from *Darkness on the Edge of Town*, five from *Born to Run*, the perennial set closer "Rosalita" from *The Wild, the Innocent & the E Street Shuffle*, plus "Fire" and

"Because the Night" from his seemingly bottomless supply of unrecorded hits. And, of course, the Mitch Ryder medley which was the highlight of the *No Nukes* LP.

But the show has that shape only on nights Springsteen hasn't declared a special occasion, which is a rare night in itself. On Halloween, the second night in L.A., he cooked up a version of "Haunted House," the old Jumpin' Gene Simmons hit, at soundcheck, and opened the set with it—after appearing from a coffin, and being chased around the stage by ghoul-robed roadies during the guitar break.

On Saturday he added an acoustic-guitar-and-accordion version of "The Price You Pay" and did "Fade Away," the one song from *The River* he'd avoided. On Monday night, with Bob Dylan in the house for a second night (he'd come with Jim Keltner on Thursday and been impressed), Springsteen put "The Price You Pay" back in and dedicated it to his "inspiration." Plus a lengthy "Growing Up," from his first album. On both nights he ended the encores with Jackson Browne, dueting on "Sweet Little Sixteen." On neither night did the inclusion of the additional songs mean the removal of any of the others.

"Yeah, but you really missed it in St. Paul," said Van Zandt. "He turned around and called 'Midnight Hour' and we all just about fainted. Funky [bassist Garry Tallent] didn't even believe we were doing it until about the second chorus." The band had not rehearsed the song and it's unlikely that the E Street Band's present lineup had ever played it before in its five years together. But even the musicians thought it sounded great.

The expansiveness and elasticity of Springsteen's shows is a conundrum, because arena rock is in all other hands the surest route to formula. One of the most miserable summers of my existence, 1975, was spent watching fifteen Rolling Stones shows. By the fifth I was fighting to stay awake; by the tenth I'd stopped fighting, a circumstance I ascribed to the band's senility until it occurred to me that no one was meant to look at more than one or maybe two of their damn fiestas.

That's rock 'n' roll for tourists. Springsteen plays for the natives. Although he would probably put it more idealistically, he's really just never lost the consciousness of a bar band musician, who knows that a good part of the house may be seeing all three sets. And like a bar band veteran, he refuses to resort to gimmicks. Mark Brickman's lighting is the best in rock, but it's based on relatively simple theatrical gels and an authoritative sense of timing with follow spots; any funk band in the Midwest might have a more elaborate concept, but nobody with lasers achieves such an effective result. (Brickman has a computer along on this tour, but only, he told me, because "if you can figure out a way to program Bruce's show, you can figure a way to make it work for anything." Most nights, Brickman and soundman Bruce Jackson might as well throw their set lists away.)

But what reveals Springsteen's bar band roots more than anything is his sense of intimacy with the crowd. One night during this tour, someone told me, he actually announced from the stage, "If the guy I met at the airport yesterday is here, please come to the stage at the break. I've got something for you," which is about as close to sock-hop mentality as you could ask. In Phoenix, during "Rosalita," Bruce made one of his patented leaps to the speakers at the side of the stage. But this time he missed. The crowd just kept cheering, but back at the soundboard the tension was thick. Bruce might do anything, but this was weird, the band was holding the chord, and the chords of "Rosalita" are not meant to be held for five seconds, much less fifteen.

It's a good long drop from the top of the speakers, two feet high, to the floor, eight or nine feet away. All there was between Bruce and the hard concrete floor was the band's monitor mixing board, but as he tumbled down, roadie Bob Werner reached out and broke the fall (spraining his wrist in the process).

Neither the band nor the crowd could see any of this. The next thing any of us knew, the guitar appeared, tossed atop the speakers. Then a pair of hands, and at last, Springsteen's head, with his silly-faced little-boy grin. He shook his head, pulled himself the rest of the way up, strapped on his guitar, and went back into action as if nothing had occurred.

This moment is presumably on film—there was a crew shooting a commercial that night—though from what angle I cannot say. But what that incident proclaims, more than anything, even Bruce's sense of spontaneity, is his sense of event. The cardinal rule of his shows is that something always happens. It's not only, as he says in the interview that follows, that he's prepared for whatever happens; *somehow*, he always makes sure it does. I've seen at least a hundred shows in the past six or seven years. The worst was fascinating; the most awesome have been the times when, after four or five nights of hell-raising action, he manages to make it different again. This guy does not know the meaning of anticlimax.

That's the bright side. There are darker ones. In Los Angeles, where ticket scalping is legal, front-row seats were going for $180, $200, $250. And fans wrote Bruce to complain, not just that tickets were being scalped, but that the best ones were. It's an old story and most bands would let it slide, but Bruce took a stand. Each night in L.A. he gave the crowd the name of a state legislator, and radio station, who'd agreed to campaign to change the scalping law in California. This might qualify as a gesture (although the night after Jon Landau got a preshow phone call from a "ticket agent" suggesting that Bruce "do what he does, and I'll do what I do, so why don't he just lay off," he made the announcement three times). But he's also hired investigators to get to the bottom of the mess, with intentions of turning the information over to the proper authorities if any hard evidence can be turned up.

And this reflects the spirit in which Springsteen played M.U.S.E. Although he was one of only two musicians at the benefit who did not make a political statement in the concert program (the other was Tom Petty), Springsteen upstaged the issue only accidentally. He felt that particular problem to his marrow; "Roulette," the song he wrote right after Three Mile Island, is the scariest piece of music he's ever done, for my money far more frightening than even the last line of "Stolen Car," and unmistakably based on the event. There is more to come.

The River itself feels like a farewell to innocence. As Springsteen notes in the interview, the innocent characters on this album are anachronisms. Their time is gone. That guy lying by the side of the road in "Wreck on the Highway" is not only the guy in "Cadillac Ranch" and "Ramrod," he is also Spanish Johnny, the original man-child hero of *The Wild, the Innocent & the E Street Shuffle.*

The River is, I think, Bruce Springsteen's best album for this very reason. It sums up seven years of work, and it does not shy away from the errors of his career thus far, nor does it disown them. He remains a romantic and a bit of a juvenile, after all this; who but a romantic juvenile could conceive of a purposeless car thief as a genuine figure of tragedy? But he is also capable now of tying together his hopes and fears. The most joyous of songs are awash with brutal undercurrents.

The River wasn't the record anyone would have predicted Bruce Springsteen would make. Epics aren't anticipated (although they might be the subject of certain fervent hopes).

But if *The River* was unpredictable, the album that will follow it is almost unimaginable. And not only because the society that shaped Springsteen's most beloved characters and the musical tradition he cherishes is now crumbling.

Among other things, *The River* is a Number One record. "Hungry Heart" looks likely to be his first Top Ten single. Things change when that happens, and we have not yet seen the rock 'n' roller who is strong enough to withstand those changes. It would be naive to expect Bruce Springsteen to be any different.

Yet Bruce Springsteen's career is all about naive faith. Who else could have survived The New Dylan, The Future of Rock 'n' Roll, The Hype, The Boss, and emerged not only successful, but respected? It's easy to play cynical rock journalist and suppose the worst—no one else has exactly cruised through success—but the fact is, Bruce Springsteen is the only human I have ever met who cannot sell out. He doesn't have a price, because the things he wants are quite literally beyond price. You don't have to believe me. Just wait and see. As Miami Steve says, "For the first time, I can really imagine rock 'n' roll at forty."

The interview below took place at the Fiesta Motel in Tempe, Arizona, on November 6 from about three-thirty A.M. until dawn. (The time frame is typical.) Bruce had just completed a show at Arizona State University, and in a strange way, what I'll remember about the night isn't talking with him or even the fall off the speakers but the lines he sang just after the fall, that climactic verse of "Rosalita."

> *Tell your daddy this is his last chance*
> *If he wants his daughter to have some fun*
> *Because my brand new record, Rosie*
> *Just came in at Number One*

He won't forget, either.

MUSICIAN: *Here you are,* The River *is a Number One album, the single is a hit, you're playing great shows in the biggest halls and selling them out. In a sense, a lot of goals you must have had are now achieved. What goals are left?*

SPRINGSTEEN: Doing it is the goal. It's not to play some big place, or for a record to be Number One. Doing it is the end, not the means. That's the point. So the point is: What's next? Some more of this.

But bigness—that is no end. That, as an end, is meaningless, essentially. It's good, 'cause you can reach a lotta people, and that's the idea. The idea was just to go out and to reach people. And after tonight, you go out and you reach more people and then the night after that, you do that again.

MUSICIAN: *One of the things that* The River *and also the show, its length and certain of the things you say between songs, are about is seeing more possibilities, more opportunities for things to do.*

SPRINGSTEEN: Yeah. There's an immense amount, and I'm just starting to get some idea about what I want to do. Because we've been in a situation, always, until recently, there's been a lot of instability in everybody's life. The band's and mine. It dates back to the very beginning, from the bars on up to even after we were successful. Then there was the lawsuit.

And then there's the way we work, which is, we're *slow.* And in the studio, I'm slow. I take a long time. That means you spend a lotta money in the studio. Not only do you spend a lotta money, you don't make any money, because you're out of the stream of things. It's like you can never get ahead, because as soon as you get ahead, you stop for two years and you go back to where you were.

MUSICIAN: *Is that slowness as frustrating for you as it is for everybody else?*

SPRINGSTEEN: I'm lucky, because I'm in there, I'm seeing it every step of the way. I would assume that if you didn't know what was going on, and you cared about it, it would be frustrating. With me, it was not frustrating.

You know, we started to work on the album and I had a certain idea at the beginning. And at the end, that was the idea that came out on the record. It took a very long time, all the coloring and stuff, there was a lot of decisions and songs to be written. Right up until the very last two weeks, when I rewrote the last two verses to "Point Blank." "Drive All Night" was done just the week before that. Those songs didn't exist, in the form that they're on the record, until the last few weeks we were in the studio. So there's stuff happening all the time. But we get into that little bit of a cycle, which hopefully we'll be able to break—maybe. I don't know.

MUSICIAN: *In a lot of ways,* The River *feels like the end of a cycle. Certain ideas that began with the second and third albums have matured, and a lot of the contrasts and contradictions have been, not resolved, but they've been heightened.*

SPRINGSTEEN: On this album, I just said, "I don't understand all these things. I don't see where all these things fit. I don't see how all these things can work together." It was because I was always focusing in on some small thing; when I stepped back, they made a sense of their own. It was just a situation of living with all those contradictions. And that's what happens. There's never any making ends meet or finding any time of long-standing peace of mind about something.

MUSICIAN: *That's sort of like "Wreck on the Highway," where, for the first time in your songs, you've got the night-mare and the dream in the same package.*

SPRINGSTEEN: That was a funny song. I wrote that song real fast, in one night. We came in and played a few takes of it and that's pretty much what's on the album, I think. That's an automatic song, a song that you don't really think about, or work on. You just look back and it sorta surprises you.

MUSICIAN: *On this record, it also feels like you're relying a lot more on your instincts, the sort of things that happen onstage.*

SPRINGSTEEN: Yeah, that's what happens the most to make the record different. A lot of it is real instinctive. "Hungry Heart" I wrote in a half hour, or ten minutes, real fast. All the rockers—"Crush on You," "You Can Look," "Ramrod"—were all written very quickly, from what I can remember. "Wreck on the Highway" was; "Stolen Car" was. Most of the songs were, sit down and write 'em. There weren't any songs where I worked—"Point Blank" I did, but actually those last two verses I wrote pretty quickly. "The River" took a while. I had the verses, I never had any chorus, and I didn't have no title for a long time.

MUSICIAN: *But you always had the basic arrangement?*

SPRINGSTEEN: No, on that song I had these verses, and I was fooling around with the music. What gave me the idea for the title was a Hank Williams song. I think it's "My Bucket Got a Hole in It," where he goes down to the river to jump in and kill himself, and he can't because it dried up. So I was just sitting there one night, thinking, and I just thought about this song. "My Bucket's Got a Hole in It" and that's where I got the chorus. [Actually, Springsteen is thinking of "Long Gone Lonesome Blues."]

I love that old country music. All during the last tour that's what I listened to a whole lot—I listened to Hank Williams. I went back and dug up all his first sessions, the gospel kind of stuff that he did. That and the first real

Johnny Cash record with "Give My Love to Rose," "I Walk the Line," "Hey Porter," "Six Foot High and Risin'," "I Don't Like It But I Guess Things Happen That Way." That and the rockabilly.

There was a certain something in all that stuff that just seemed to fit in with things that I was thinking about, or worrying about. Especially the Hank Williams stuff. He always has all that conflict, he always has that real religious side, and the honky tonkin', all that side. There's a great song, "Settin' the Woods on Fire." That thing is outrageous. That's "Ramrod," that had some of that in it. And "Cadillac Ranch."

MUSICIAN: *Earlier, you said that "Ramrod" was one of the saddest things you'd written. Why?*

SPRINGSTEEN: [*laughs*] Well, it's so anachronistic, you know. The character—it's impossible, what he wants to do. One of the ideas of it, when I wrote it, it was sort of like a partner to "Cadillac Ranch" and a few things, it's got the old big engine sound. That song is a goddamn gas guzzler [*laughing*]. And that was the sound I wanted, that big, rumbling, big engine sound. And this guy, he's there, but he's really *not* there no more. He's the guy in "Wreck on the Highway"—either guy, actually. But he's also the guy, in the end, who says, "I'll give you the word, now, sugar, we'll go ramroddin' forevermore." I don't know, that's a real sad line to me, sometimes.

MUSICIAN: *If you believe it, you mean.*

SPRINGSTEEN: Yeah, but it's a funny kinda thing. I love it when we play that song onstage. It's just a happy song, a celebration of all that stuff that's gonna be gone—is gone already, almost.

I threw that song ten million times off the record. Ten million times. I threw it off *Darkness* and I threw it off this one, too. Because I thought it was wrong.

MUSICIAN: *You mentioned something similar about "Out in the Street," that it was too much of a fantasy to possibly believe it.*

SPRINGSTEEN: I was just wary of it at the time, I guess for some of the same reasons. It always seemed anachronistic, and at the time, I was demanding of all the songs that they be able to translate. All the characters, they're part of the past, they're part of the future, and they're part of the present. And I guess there was a certain frightening aspect to seeing one that wasn't part of the future. He was part of the past.

To me, that was the conflict of that particular song. I loved it, we used to play it all the time. And there was that confusion, too. Well, if I love playing the damn thing so much, why the hell don't I want to put it on the record?

I guess I always made sure that the characters always had that foot planted up ahead somewhere. Not just the one back there. That's what makes 'em viable, or real today. But I also knew a lotta people who were exactly like this. So I said, "Well, that's okay." There was just a point where I said, "That's okay," to a lot of things where I previously would not have said so.

I gained a certain freedom in making the two-record set, because I could let all those people out that usually I'd put away. Most of the time, they'd end up being my favorite songs, and probably some of my best songs, you know.

MUSICIAN: *You mean the kind of songs that would show up onstage but not on record? ["Fire," "Because the Night," "Sherry Darling"]*

SPRINGSTEEN: Yeah, I'm the kind of person, I think a lot about everything. Nothin' I can do about it. It's like, I'm a thinkin' fool. That's a big part of me. Now, the other part is, I can get onstage and cut that off and be superinstinctive. To be a good live performer, you have to be instinctive. It's like, to walk in the jungle, or to do anything where there's

56

a certain tightrope wire aspect, you need to be instinctive. And you have to be comfortable at it also.

Like tonight, I was falling on my head. I wasn't worrying about it. I just went, it just happened [*laughs*]. You just think, what happens next? When I was gonna jump on that speaker, I couldn't worry about whether I was gonna make it or not. You can't. You just gotta do it. And if you do, you do, and if you don't, you don't, and then something else happens. That's the point of the live performance.

Now, when I get into the studio, both things operate. When we perform on this record, I feel that we have that thing going that we've got live. To me, we're not rockin' that stuff better live than a lot of it is on the record. I can still listen to it. Usually, two weeks after we're out on the record, I cannot listen to my record anymore. 'Cause as soon as I hear some crappy tape off the board, it sounds ten times better than what we spent all that time doing in the studio. This is the very first album that I've been able to go back and put on to play, and it sounds good to me.

But in the studio I'm conceptual. I have a self-consciousness. And there's a point where I often would try to stop that. "No, that's bad. Look at all these great records, and I betcha they didn't think about it like this, or think about it this long." You realize that it doesn't matter. That's unimportant, it's ridiculous. I got into a situation where I just said, "Hey, this is what I do, and these are my assets and these are my burdens." I got comfortable with myself being that kind of person.

MUSICIAN: *But only after going to extremes.* Darkness *is the least spontaneous of your records.*

SPRINGSTEEN: That's right. And it's funny because "Darkness on the Edge of Town," that cut is live in the studio. "Streets of Fire" is live in the studio, essentially. "Factory" is live. It's not a question of how you actually do it. The idea is to sound spontaneous, not be spontaneous.

So at this point, I just got settled into accepting certain things that I've always been uncomfortable with. I stopped setting limits and definitions—which I always threw out anyway, but which I'd always feel guilty about. Spending a long time in the studio, I stopped feeling bad about that, I said, "That's me, that's what I do." I work slow, and I work slow for a reason: to get the results I want.

When you try to define what makes a good rock 'n' roll record, or what is rock 'n' roll, everyone has their own personal definition. But when you put limits on it, you're just throwing stuff away.

MUSICIAN: *Isn't one of your definitions that it's limitless?*

SPRINGSTEEN: I think it is. That's my definition, I guess. Hey, you can go out in the street and do the twist and that's rock 'n' roll. It's the moment, it's all things [*laughs*]. It's funny, to me, it just is.

You know, my music utilizes things from the past, because that's what the past is for. It's to learn from. It's not to limit you, you shouldn't be limited by it, which I guess was one of my fears on "Ramrod." I don't want to make a record like they made in the Fifties or the Sixties or the Seventies. I want to make a record like today, that's right now.

To do that, I go back, back further all the time. Back into Hank Williams, back into Jimmie Rodgers. Because the human thing in those records, that should be at least the heart of it. The human thing that's in those records is just beautiful and awesome. I put on that Hank Williams and Jimmie Rodgers stuff, and wow! What inspiration! It's got that beauty and the purity. The same thing with a lot of the great Fifties records, and the early rockabilly. I went back and dug up all the early rockabilly stuff because . . . what mysterious people they were.

There's this song, "Jungle Rock" by Hank Mizell. *Where*

is Hank Mizell? What happened to him? What a mysterious person, what a ghost. And you put that thing on and you can see him. You can see him standing in some little studio, way back when, and just singing that song. No reason [*laughs*]. Nothing gonna come out of it. Didn't sell. That wasn't no Number One record, and he wasn't playin' no big arena after it, either.

But what a moment, what a mythic moment, what a mystery. Those records are filled with mystery, they're shrouded with mystery. Like these wild men came out from somewhere, and man, they were so alive. The joy and the abandon. Inspirational, inspirational records, those records.

MUSICIAN: *You mentioned earlier that when you went into the arenas you were worried about losing certain things.*

SPRINGSTEEN: I was afraid maybe it would screw up the range of artistic expression that the band had. Because of the lack of silence. A couple of things happened. Number one, it's a rock 'n' roll show. People are gonna scream their heads off whenever they feel like it. That's fine—happens in theaters, happens in clubs [*laughs*]. Doesn't matter where the hell it is, happens every place, and that's part of it, you know.

On this tour it's been really amazing, because we've been doing all those real quiet songs. And we've been able to do 'em. And then we've been able to rock real hard and get that thing happening from the audience. I think part of the difference is that the demands that are made on the audience now are much heavier, much heavier on the audience that sees us now than on the last tour.

But the moment you begin to depend on audience reaction, you're doing the wrong thing. You're doin' it wrong, it's a mistake, it's not right. You can't allow yourself, no matter what, to depend on them. I put that mike out to the crowd, you have a certain faith that somebody's gonna yell somethin' back. Some nights it's louder than other nights and some nights they do, and on some songs they don't. But that's the idea. I think when you begin to expect a reaction, it's a mistake. You gotta have your thing completely together—boom!—right there with you. That's what makes nights special and what makes nights different from other nights.

MUSICIAN: *On the other hand, the only way to do a really perfect show is to involve that audience. Maybe an audience only gets lazy if the performer doesn't somehow keep it on its toes.*

SPRINGSTEEN: I'm out there for a good time and to be inspired at night, and to play with my band and to rock those songs as hard as we can rock 'em. I think that you can have some of the best nights under the very roughest conditions. A lotta times, at Max's or some of the clubs in Jersey, they'd be sittin' on their hands or nobody wants to dance, and the adversity is a positive motivation.

The only concern is that what's being done is being done the way it should be done. The rest you don't have control over. But I think that our audience is the best audience in the world. The amount of freedom that I get from the crowd is really a lot.

MUSICIAN: *The way the stage show is organized is that the first half is about work and struggling, the second half is about joy, release, transcending a lot of those things in the first half. Is that conscious?*

SPRINGSTEEN: I knew that I wanted a certain feeling for the first set. That's sorta the way it stacks up.

MUSICIAN: *What you rarely get a sense of around rock bands is work, especially rock 'n' roll as a job of work. Yet around this band, you can't miss it.*

SPRINGSTEEN: That's at the heart of the whole thing. There's a beauty in work and I love it, all different kinds of work. That's what I consider it. This is my job, and that's my work. And I work my ass off, you know.

MUSICIAN: *In Los Angeles one night, when you introduced "Factory," you made a distinction between two different kinds of work. Do you remember what it was?*

SPRINGSTEEN: There's people that get a chance to do the kind of work that changes the world, and make things really different. And then there's the kind that just keeps the world from falling apart. And that was the kind that my dad always did. 'Cause we were always together as a family, and we grew up in a . . . good situation, where we had what we needed. And there was a lot of sacrifice on his part and my mother's part for that to happen. . . .

MUSICIAN: The River *has a lot of those sorts of workers—the people in "Jackson Cage," the guy in "The River" itself.*

SPRINGSTEEN: I never knew anybody who was unhappy with their job and was happy with their life. It's your sense of purpose. Now, some people can find it elsewhere. Some people can work a job and find it someplace else.

MUSICIAN: *Like the character in "Racing in the Street"?*

SPRINGSTEEN: Yeah. But I don't know if that's lasting. But people do, they find ways.

MUSICIAN: *Or else . . . ?*

SPRINGSTEEN: [*long pause*] Or else they join the Ku Klux Klan or something. That's where it can take you, you know. It can take you a lot of strange places.

MUSICIAN: *Introducing "Factory" on a different night, you spoke about your father having been real angry, and then, after a while, not being angry anymore. "He was just silent." Are you still angry?*

SPRINGSTEEN: I don't know. I don't know. I don't know if I know myself that well. I think I know myself a lot, but

I'm not sure [*laughs*]. It's impossible not to be angry when you see the state of things and look around. You have to be somewhat.

MUSICIAN: *Tonight, you were saying onstage that you found the election terrifying. That seems to go hand in hand with playing the M.U.S.E. benefits, and striking back at ticket scalpers in L.A. You wouldn't have done those things two years ago, I don't think. Are you finding social outlets for that anger now?*

SPRINGSTEEN: That's true. It's just a whole values thing. Take the ticket thing. It's a hustle. And a hustle has become . . . respected. In a lot of quarters—on a street level, dope pushers—it's a respectable thing to hustle somebody. I mean, how many times in the Watergate thing did people say about Nixon, "Well, he just wasn't smart enough to get away with it"? And there's a certain point where people have become cynical, where the hustle, that's the American way. I think it's just turned upside down in a real bad way. I think it should lose its respect.

MUSICIAN: *Do you feel that way about nuclear energy?*

SPRINGSTEEN: It's just the whole thing, it's the whole thing. It's terrible, it's horrible. Somewhere along the way, the idea, which I think was initially to get some fair transaction between people, went out the window. And what came in was the most you can get [*laughs*]. The most you can get and the least you can give. That's why cars are the way they are today. It's just an erosion of all the things that were true and right about the original idea.

MUSICIAN: *But that isn't something that was on your mind much until the* Darkness *album?*

SPRINGSTEEN: Up to then, I didn't think about too many things. In *Greetings from Asbury Park*, I did. And then I went off a little bit, and sort of roundabout came back to it.

I guess it just started after *Born to Run* somehow. We were off for three years, and home for a long time. It came out of a local kind of thing—what my old friends were doing, what my relatives were doing. How things were affecting them, and what their lives were like. And what my life was like.

MUSICIAN: *Did you have a sense that no one else was telling that story?*

SPRINGSTEEN: I didn't see it too much, except in the English stuff. Things were being addressed that way in that stuff.

MUSICIAN: *You mean, for instance, the Clash?*

SPRINGSTEEN: Yeah, all that kinda stuff. I liked it. I always liked that stuff. But there wasn't too much stuff in America happening. It just seemed to me that's the story. But there was a crucial level of things missing, and it is today still. Maybe it's just me getting older and seeing things more as they are.

MUSICIAN: *On* Darkness, *the character's response is to isolate himself from any community, and try to beat the system on his own. The various characters on* The River *are much more living in the mainstream of society.*

SPRINGSTEEN: That guy at the end of *Darkness* has reached a point where you just have to strip yourself of everything, to get yourself together. For a minute, sometimes, you just have to get rid of everything, just to get yourself together inside, be able to push everything away. And I think that's what happened at the end of the record.

And then there was the thing where the guy comes back.

MUSICIAN: *And* The River *is what he sees?*

SPRINGSTEEN: Yeah, these are his feelings, it's pretty much there, and in the shows it's there now, too, I guess. I hate to get too literal about it, because I can never explain it as well as when I wrote about it. I hate to limit it. I look back at *Darkness* or the other records, and there were things going on that I never knew were going on.

MUSICIAN: *Do you like* Born to Run *or* Darkness *better now?*

SPRINGSTEEN: Not particularly. On *Darkness*, I like the ideas, I'm not crazy about the performances. We play all those songs ten times better live. But I like the idea. *Born to Run*, I like the performances and the sound. Sometimes it sounds funny.

MUSICIAN: *Young and innocent?*

SPRINGSTEEN: Yeah, yeah. Same thing with *The Wild and the Innocent*. I have a hard time listening to any of those records. Certain things on each record I can listen to: "Racing in the Street," "Backstreets," "Prove It All Night," "Darkness on the Edge of Town." But not a lot, because either the performance doesn't sound right to me, or the ideas sound like a long time ago.

MUSICIAN: *Do you remember when you threw the birthday cake into the crowd, at the second M.U.S.E. concert?*

SPRINGSTEEN: [*laughs*] Oh, yeah. That was a wild night.

MUSICIAN: *You'd just turned thirty that night, and didn't seem to be overjoyed by it. But a couple of weeks ago in Cleveland, I was kidding Danny about turning thirty and said, "Oh, yeah, we're thirty now, can't do what we used to do." You said, real quick, "That's not true." What happened in that year? Was that significant, turning thirty?*

SPRINGSTEEN: I don't remember. It just made me wanna do more things. I think, as a matter of fact, when we were in the studio, that was the thing that was big. I didn't feel we were going too slow for what we were doing. But I felt that I wanted to be quicker just to have more time. I wanted to be touring, for one thing. I wanted to be touring *right now*.

MUSICIAN: *But by the time you finish this tour, you'll be crowding thirty-two. Then, if you're right and it's just gonna take a year or so to make a record, you'll be thirty-three or*

64

thirty-four by the time you get out again. Can you still have the stamina to do the kind of show you feel you need to do?

SPRINGSTEEN: Who knows? I'm sure it'll be a different type of show. It's impossible to tell and a waste of time guessin'.

When I was in the studio and wanted to play, it wasn't the way I felt in a physical kind of way, it was what I felt mentally. I was excited about the record and I wanted to play those songs live. I wanted to get out there and travel around the world with people who were my friends. And see every place and play just as hard as we could play, every place in the world. Just get into things, see things, see what happens.

MUSICIAN: *Like in "Badlands"?*

SPRINGSTEEN: That's it. That's the idea. I want to see what happens, what's next. All I knew when I was in the studio, sometimes, was that I felt great that day. And I was wishing I was somewhere strange, playing. I guess that's the thing I love doing the most. And it's the thing that makes me feel most alert and alive.

MUSICIAN: *You look awful before a show, and then those hours up there, which exhaust everyone else, refresh you.*

SPRINGSTEEN: I always look terrible before the show. That's when I feel worst. And after the show, it's like a million bucks. Simple as that. You feel a little tired, but you never feel better. Nothing makes me feel as good as those hours between when you walk offstage, until I go to bed. That's the hours that I live for. As feelings go, that's ten on a scale of ten. I just feel like talking to people, going out back and meeting those kids, doing any damn thing. Most times I just come back and eat and lay down and feel good. Most people, I don't think, get to feel that good, doing whatever they do.

MUSICIAN: *You can't get that in the studio?*

SPRINGSTEEN: Sometimes, but it's different. You get wired for two or three days or a week or so and then sometimes, you feel real low. I never feel as low, playing, as I do in the studio.

You know, I just knew that's what I wanted to do—go all over and play. See people and go all over the world. I want to see what all those people are like. I want to meet people from all different countries and stuff.

MUSICIAN: *You've always liked to have a certain mobility, a certain freedom of movement. Can you still walk down the street?*

SPRINGSTEEN: Oh, sure, sure. It depends where you go. Usually . . . you can do anything you want to do. The idea that you can't walk down the street is in people's minds. You can walk down any street, any time. What you gonna be afraid of, someone coming up to you? In general, it's not that different than it ever was, except you meet people you ordinarily might not meet—you meet some strangers and you talk to 'em for a little while.

The other night I went out, I went driving, we were in Denver. Got a car and went out, drove all around. Went to the movies by myself, walked in, got my popcorn. This guy comes up to me, real nice guy. He says, "Listen, you want to sit with me and my sister?" I said, "All right." So we watch the movie [*laughs*]. It was great, too, because it was that Woody Allen movie [*Stardust Memories*], the guy's slammin' to his fans. And I'm sittin' there and this poor kid says, "Jesus, I don't know what to say to ya. Is this the way it is? Is that how you feel?" I said, "No, I don't feel like that so much." And he had the amazing courage to come up to me at the end of the movie, and ask if I'd go home and meet his mother and father. I said, "What time is it?" It was eleven o'clock, so I said, "Well, okay."

So I go home with him, he lives out in some suburb. So we get over to the house and here's his mother and father, laying out on the couch, watching TV and reading the paper. He brings me in and he says, "Hey, I got Bruce Springsteen here." And they don't believe him. So he pulls me over, and he says, "This is Bruce Springsteen." "Aw, g'wan," they say. So he runs in his room and brings out an album and he holds it up to my face. And his mother says [*breathlessly*] "Ohh, *yeah!*" She starts yelling, "Yeah!" she starts screaming.

And for two hours I was in this kid's house, talking with these people, they were really nice, they cooked me up all this food, watermelon, and the guy gave me a ride home a few hours later.

I felt so good that night. Because here are these strange people I didn't know, they take you in their house, treat you fantastic, and this kid was real nice, they were real nice. That is something that can happen to me that can't happen to most people. And when it does happen, it's fantastic. You get somebody's whole life in three hours. You get their parents, you get their sister, you get their family life, in three hours. And I went back to that hotel and felt really good because I thought, "Wow [*almost whispering*], what a thing to be able to do. What an experience to be able to have, to be able to step into some stranger's life."

And that's what I thought about in the studio. I thought about going out and meeting people I don't know. Going to France and Germany and Japan, and meeting Japanese people and French people, and German people. Meeting them and seeing what they think, and being able to go over there with something. To go over with a pocketful of ideas or to go over there with just something, to be able to take something over. And boom! To do it.

But you can't do one without the other. I couldn't do it if I hadn't spent time in the studio, knowing what I say and what I feel right now.

MUSICIAN: *Because then you wouldn't have that pocket-ful of ideas?*

SPRINGSTEEN: Then, if you don't have that, stay home or something. If you have some ideas to exchange, that's what it's about. That's at the heart of it. I just wouldn't go out and tour unless I had that. There wouldn't be a reason.

The reason is you have some idea you wanna say. You have an idea about things, an opinion, a feeling about the way things are or the way things could be. You wanna go out and tell people about it. You wanna tell people, "Well, if everybody did this or if people thought this, maybe it would be better."

When we play the long show, that's because it gives the whole picture. And if you aren't given the whole picture, you're not gonna get the whole picture. We play the first part . . . that first part is about those things that you said it was about. That's the foundation; without that the rest couldn't happen. Wouldn't be no second half without the first half, couldn't be all them other things, without those things. Without that foundation of the hard things, and the struggling things, the work thing. That's the heart, that's what it comes down to.

And then on top of that, there's the living, the things that surround that. That's why the show's so long. "You wanna leave out 'Stolen Car'?" No, that's a little part of the puzzle. "You wanna leave this out?" No, that's a little part of the puzzle. And at the end, if you want, you can look back and see . . . just a point of view, really. You see somebody's idea, the way somebody sees things. And you know somebody.

People go to that show, they know me. They know a lotta me, as much as I know that part of myself. That's why, when I meet 'em on the street, they know you already.

And you know them, too. Because of their response.

MUSICIAN: *Even these days, it's still not very far from the dressing room to the stage for you, is it?*

SPRINGSTEEN: I don't know if it is. I don't know if it should be. I don't know for sure how different the thing is or how it's perceived. Except a lot of the music is real idealistic, and I guess like anybody else, you don't live up to it all the time. You just don't. That's the challenge. You got to walk it like you talk it. That's the idea. That's the line. I guess that's pretty much what it's about.

THE E STREET BAND'S EQUIPMENT

Bruce Springsteen

Guitars: 1954 Esquire, modified with extra Telecaster pickup (*the* guitar); 1956 Telecaster (spare); 1954 Telecaster (spare); Ovation six-string acoustic; two Rickenbacker twelve-string electrics; 1958 Gibson J-200 acoustic (same as Elvis's original, and was a gift from crew members Mike Batlan, Marc Brickman, and Bob Chirmside). *Amps:* Four Fender Bassman amps, circa 1958–1962; two Peavey Vintage amps (imitation Bassmans) — one of each is used onstage under the drum riser. Also, a Prime Time digital delay and harmonizer and an MXR distortion box. The Fender Esquire is modified with a battery-operated impedance transformer for long cable lengths. There is an asterisk in front of the Esquire's serial number, indicating that it was a factory reject, probably originally sold as a reject.

Miami Steve Van Zandt

MUSICIAN: *What equipment do you use onstage?*

VAN ZANDT: I don't know, you've gotta ask Dougie (Sutphin, E Street roadie).

69

MUSICIAN: *When was the last time you did know?*

VAN ZANDT: In '65, I bought a Telecaster, and that's the last thing I remember.

MUSICIAN: *But lately, you've begun to use those Ovation twelve-strings onstage. . . .*

VAN ZANDT: I went to [actor] Sal Viscuso's house here in L.A., and he had homemade pasta, homemade bracciola, he had provolone and mozzarella flown in from New York. And the strangest thing happened: I went home and dreamed I was Leadbelly with an Italian accent.

MUSICIAN: *So not paying attention to the technical details doesn't have much effect on your sound?*

VAN ZANDT: No, I'll tell you, I've got a secret technique. I play everything at ten. That's the great equalizer. You'd be surprised how similar everything sounds when you do that.

Musician eventually did track down Doug Sutphin, doing laps at Malibu Grand Prix. At a pit stop, Sutphin informed us that Van Zandt has two Stratocasters, a '57 and a '67, a Gibson Firebird (a spare which he almost never plays onstage), and two hollow-body twelve-string Ovation guitars, with pickups. One of the Ovations and one of the Strats is capoed. Van Zandt has a Mesa Boogie amp with Electro-Voice speakers, two Roland Jazz Choirs (120) amps, and a hundred-watt Hi Watt brain and cabinet, plux an MXR distortion unit. And yes, he does play it all at ten.

Clarence Clemons

The Big Man plays Selver Mark VI tenors (a whole bunch of 'em) and altos and Yamaha baritones and sopranos, with La-Voz reeds and Berg Larson mouthpieces. He uses a variety of percussion (claves, tambourines, cowbell, etc.) and maracas by the Argentine Hernandez company. His horns are miked with a device invented by Clemons and Bruce Jackson.

Roy Bittan

Bittan, who's almost as well known for his session playing (with Meat Loaf, Dire Straits, and others) as for his work with the E Street crew, uses a Yamaha C-7 grand piano as his basic instrument. He also plays a Yamaha CS80 synthesizer on a couple of numbers. The piano is fitted with a modified Helpinstill pickup. "The most important thing," the Professor says, "is ten fingers and fast hands."

Danny Federici

Danny Federici is surrounded by banks of equipment onstage, which is unfortunate, since it tends to obscure some of the fanciest footwork in human history. While dancing, Federici plays a Hammond B-3 organ (with a spare backstage — one of them was cut down by John Stilwell of Ithaca, New York), two Farfisa combo compacts, and an Acetone (Top 5 model), used exclusively for "Wreck on the Highway." The sound is channeled through two customized Leslies with 12 two-inch speakers, Gauss HF 4000 horn drivers and IF fifteen-inch speakers, and speed relays for both. Federici's amp rack, designed by Sound Specialties of Philadelphia, holds a Marantz 510 MR (600 watts) for the low end, a Phase Linear 400 for the horns, a Urei 521 crossover system, a Bi-Amp Model 270 graphic equalizer, and a Roland RU100 reverb unit. Danny also plays a keyboard-operated glockenspiel, which is, he thinks, one of only two or three in the world. (When the E Streeters toured England and Scandinavia in '75, they managed to find one to complement his pair.) That runs through a standard Leslie 122 mounted in an Anvil case with an acoustic chamber and permanent mikes for offstage miking.

Federici's organ modifications (B3 cutdown, speed switches and relays) were done by John Stilwell and Springsteen soundman Bruce Jackson.

Max Weinberg

The Mighty Max, as he's introduced nightly, brought to his drum list as highly developed a sense of detail as he brings to his playing. He uses a twenty-four-by-fourteen-inch Ludwig six-ply bass with an Emperor head and fourteen coats of white varnish; it's stuffed with two old down pillows and miked with a Beyer 88.

Weinberg's toms are also Ludwigs, a ten-by-fourteen-inch and a sixteen-by-sixteen-inch. The rack tom has Countryman contact mikes taped to the inside shell and a Sennheiser 421 mike for the top head. The floor tom is miked with just the 421. The toms are slightly muffled with Green Bay paper towels — Weinberg insists on that brand.

His stage snare is a six-and-a-half-by-fourteen-inch Pearl snare with a Diplomat snare head and a Durotone batter head, miked inside with a Countryman, outside with a Shure SM81 and another Sennheiser 421. (For recording, he prefers a black five-and-a-half-by-fourteen-inch snare.)

Weinberg plays with Pro Mark 5B sticks (no varnish), uses a Cameo Chain pedal (squared off), a Pearl Hi Hat Stand and Pearl hardware. A custom-welded roll bar holds his three Zildjian cymbals (eighteen-inch crash, twenty-one-inch ride, and twenty-inch medium thin crash), mikes (AKG451 EB CK-1 Cart and three Countrymen), and snare — this eliminates mike and cymbal stands.

"I've got four drums," says Weinberg. "Anything more is redundant. Besides, I tend to trip over things."

Garry Tallent

"I use a Music Man bass, with four strings (two of which I seldom use), D'Addario half-rounds. The only modification is a can of black lacquer. I've got a Countryman direct box, which is what everybody hears. Plus my own special Funky setup, which I've thought about long and hard for two years. It includes a solid-state amplifier, Acoustic 320, with an equalizer that I never use, and four Music Man bass cabinets with fifteen-inch Lansings, which I never hear. The rest is up to God and Bruce Jackson."

February 1981

U 2 :

SCENES FROM A CRUSADE

BY FRED
SCHRUERS

Stumpy, princely Bono Vox

drives along Dublin Bay, left arm grasping the wheel

of his humble sedan while the right—temporarily

game from a muscle pull he suffered pressing the flesh

with a frenzied crowd of punters near the close of a

show last week—sketches illustrations in the air. He's

describing U2's most perilous day onstage, playing be-

fore thousands of boozing poor people at Dublin's In-

ner City Festival. "This was in the open air at a place

called Sheriff Street, where they don't let the police

come around—the kids are on the roofs of these high-rise projects with crossbows. Our tour manager had told us, 'I'm advising you not to play; I'm advising the crew not to go.' They were dismantling our equipment truck before we stopped it."

U2 and their crew voted, keeping in mind Bono's admonition that canceling, with the crowd already gathered, could mean a hellish riot. They decided to go on, even after an inebriated local woman walked off a rooftop and was carted away. They set to playing, winning hearts and minds by degrees as the locals clambered on and around the stage. Finally, "This guy who looked six feet wide, a docker, just walked onstage and stood in front of me. 'Let's twist again like we did last summer,' he said. 'Play it.'

"The whole crowd quieted. This was the confrontation: Were we chicken or not? I must admit, I was chicken. I just stopped the show and started to sing, no accompaniment, 'Let's twist again, like we did last summer . . .' And I looked at the crowd, and all the kids, the mothers, fathers, the wine and whiskey bottles in their hands, started singing and dancing. And the guy smiled."

This is Bono's favorite kind of tale. He likes the smaller victories. The time the band wasn't "bottled" off the stage in Arizona, despite the promoter's warning that the kids there didn't like opening acts. The 1976 showcase gig at the Hope & Anchor Pub in London when The Edge went offstage to fix a broken string and the rest of the band, fed up with the record-biz crowd, followed him off and sat down. The overzealous moment in Birmingham when Bono, The Edge, and bassist Adam Clayton simultaneously jumped into the crowd, guitar cords popping out of the amps. . . .

Their preferred turf, in Dublin, is the dockside poets' walk known as Lazy Acre. For their "Gloria" video, the band set up on a barge moored in the middle of a dogleg inlet called the Grand Canal, safely across from a cheering crowd of kids and only a stone's throw from home base, Windmill Lane Studios. There, inside of what looks like a drab stone warehouse, is a state-of-the-art audio/video facility. We rattle past the studio, past the Docker's Pub, where the band often huddles in the "cozy" (refuge for drinking men's wives in unemancipated days) to pull on jars of creamy Guinness stout.

Winter days tend to be mild here, and even as chilling buffets of wind send the seagulls pinwheeling off course in their glide paths along the River Liffey, the scattered palm trees rising out of the loamy grass along the roadway give Dublin's center a slightly giddy, tropical air. A typical day here brings nothing more bloody than a rugby match. "No, there's no bombs going off here," says Bono, as we pass the Guinness tankers being pumped full of Liverpool's stout ration at dockside. "But there may be some getting made here. . . ."

THE HOME FRONT

The conflict in Northern Ireland is part of what goaded Bono and his bandmates to call their new record *War*, but the concept is not entirely military: "Sunday Bloody Sunday" is not so much about the Sabbath-day bloodlettings of 1920 (in Dublin) and 1972 (in Londonderry) as it is about "the trench we build within our hearts"; "New Year's Day" was inspired by Poland's beleaguered Solidarity movement, and the accompanying video uses stock footage of fighting on the Russian front in World War II, but the song also evokes lovers' separations; "Surrender" deals with suicide in Manhattan. Bono wrote "A Day Without Me" (on *Boy*, their debut) partly in reaction to the news that Joy Division's Ian Curtis had taken his own life. Since then, a school chum of Bono's, having survived electroconvulsive therapy in a Dublin institution (*Boy*'s "The Electric Co.") has "had a go at himself with an electric saw. He told me that there's only two ways out of the place—either over the wall or just to cut his throat." While visiting that friend during his recuperation, Bono was approached by a second acquaintance from his old school, who informed him the world was going to end on April Fool's Day, 1983. "I'm going through the wilderness now," he said, "but I'm coming into my glory soon. I've picked a good day for the end of the world." Bono summons up the barest of grins. "You've got to laugh. But it's disturbing, and I feel like there's a high level of mental illness in this country. And I think there's a link between that and a kind of spiritual unrest."

This spiritual unrest is hardly alien to Bono himself. The Bono who wrote an entire album as an excursion "into the heart of a child" bade good-bye to an emotionally troubled boyhood only to make *October* by virtually speaking in tongues, raging into the microphone for days on end inside an isolation booth hastily erected of corrugated iron. "Having had my notebook stolen in Seattle a few weeks before, I had no lyrics written down. So I just tried to pull out of myself what was really going on in the songs. The things you are most deeply concerned about, lying there in your subconscious, may come out in tears, or temper, or an act of violence. . . ."

Or, in Bono's case, in a couple months of raking through his own heart and mind and spilling the results onto tapes. Steve Lillywhite, the young producer who's worked on all the U2 albums, cleared a space for the singer; out of twenty-four available tracks, he left eight open for Bono's resinous wail to resound in. "Gloria" was sung partly in a monotone derived from the recordings of Gregorian chants that U2 manager Paul McGuinness had supplied; some lyrics poured out in Latin, and when Bono dashed out of the studio for a Latin dictionary in order to translate his own disgorgings, he ran into a friend who'd studied Latin and hauled him back to translate. The English words are a supplicating howl describing the exact situation Bono found himself in: "I try—to sing this song/ I try to stand up/ But I can't find my feet. . . ."

"William Butler Yeats," says Bono, "said that once there was a period where he had nothing to say. Well, to say that is in itself a statement of truth about your situation, so *say that*. I had this feeling of everything waiting on me, and I was just naked, nothing to offer. So I went through this process of wrenching what was inside myself outside of myself."

The song that now frightens him, Bono says, is "Tomorrow." He'd originally thought that the words, with their images of a black cat waiting by the side of the road and a dreaded knock on the door, had to do with the killings in Northern Ireland. A few months ago, he realized the song was about his mother's death, which came when Bono was about thirteen. "I realized that exactly what I was talking about was the morning of her funeral, not wanting to go out to that waiting black car and be a part of it. People sometimes say *October* is a religious record, but I hate to be boxed in that way."

Bono has by now transported us to Malahide Village, a suburb just north of Dublin, where The Edge lives with his family. Edge's real name is David Evans, and his father, Garvin, moved the family from Wales to Ireland because that was where his engineering business took him. As we pull up, Bono does a fond impression of Garvin singing "If a Picture Paints a Thousand Words" at the wedding of drummer Larry Mullen's father. Garvin Evans answers the door. "Why have ya still got your suit on, Mr. Edge?" asks

Bono, gesturing toward the night sky. Mr. Edge, sharp-featured like his son, momentarily tries to look stern: "Somebody's gotta earn the crust."

U2 has by now earned considerable crust, which they and Paul McGuinness would split an even five ways if they didn't insist on pouring most of it back into their own recording (thereby retaining creative control) and touring. Their second American tour campaign supporting *October* was long, hard, and costly. But they were determined to find their U.S. audience, and it seemed radio was not ready to help. So they broke one of their rules and took second billing to the J. Geils Band (brought in by Geils singer Peter Wolf) for the exposure. Even though they had virtually no time off from their 1979 signing until Bono's honeymoon last August, the band refuses to complain. They have a mission, and are decidedly unified in their determination. "When people ask us what our influences are," says Bono, "we always say, 'Each other.' "

CAMPAIGNING

My first look at U2 came in the fall of 1980, just after *Boy*'s release. Island Records publicist Neil Storey shanghaied me from the arrivals gate at Heathrow Airport directly down to Southampton College, where we walked in on U2 a few minutes before a gig. All four band members were twenty-one or younger: Larry Mullen, who organized the band by posting a notice at Mt. Temple Comprehensive School after being kicked out of the Artane Boy's (marching) Band for wearing long hair; Adam Clayton, who Bono says "couldn't even dance" at the time he picked up the bass; The Edge, who had quickly gone from acoustic noodler to budding guitar hero through a seemingly innate gift; and Bono Vox, born Paul Hewson, with the slapdash good looks and unselfconscious swagger to match his drive. "It had been a long time," recalls Dublin rock writer Bill Graham of an early U2 gig, "since I'd seen a singer who went for an audience that way, all the time watching their eyes."

Their stage show was much too large in scope for that low-ceilinged, underpopulated function room at Southampton College. The Edge's clarion calls on the treble strings, Larry's martial ferocity, and Bono's upthrust arm showed an expansive, hot-blooded streak that had been developed naturally in what Bono called "a garage band," as they went from being utter novices to playing in open market squares to the soused and skeptical local teenagers to the kind of reputation that enabled them—before they even had a contract—to fill Ireland's largest concert hall. They stood against the pretensions of the new wave's ideologues, against the "gop" on U.S. radio, against the elitism of fashion bands like Visage.

They went a long way on Bono's tirelessness, his fervor with a mike in his hand. "When you think, 'Oh, screw it, I'm not gonna climb this mountain,'" says Adam, "he's the type of person who'll hit you in the ass and get you going. It doesn't make you a lot of friends, but it's a great ability to have."

Bono gave The Edge his nickname, but he's a bit cryptic about why. When asked, he grasps Edge's long, chiseled jaw and turns it in profile: "The Edge." Then, after a pause: "Let's just say he's on the border between something and nothing."

At one point during the endless rounds of touring, Bono thought he had sussed The Edge's guitar style, and attempted to demonstrate as much at a sound check. "I'd been watching. I knew all the settings, knew his machines, the chord shapes, put my fingers where he puts his, had the volume he has it at, struck it the same way—and this *blluuug* came out of the speakers. The road crew just burst out laughing, and the guitar roadie came up and said, 'You know, I've been watching him for the past year and I've tried every day to make it sound like he does. I can't do it."

"Oh, gosh," says The Edge in his disarmingly angelic way when asked how he does it. "I tend to do something with the guitar sound, use certain effects to fatten it, rather than just use it clean—though on *War* it's cleaner than the previous two albums. I use the echo in a very concise way—I try to use the repeats in time with music. Most guitar players would use the full spectrum of the guitar to get across the power and dynamics, but by using the echo I can get away without using the bottom strings so much. I tend to use three-, maybe four-note chords rather than the full six and to use the top strings, the top end, which gives that distance between the bass and the guitar, and gives me a bit more freedom."

"We started out as nonmusicians," Bono points out. "We learned to play after the group was formed. I mean, we started to write our own material because we couldn't play other people's. Adam couldn't slap in time when he joined, Edge could play sort of bad acoustic. Larry had his military drumming, and I started singing 'cause I couldn't play guitar."

Adam Clayton concurs. "In the past, when we went in the studio, we simply didn't know our craft well enough. On *War* you can hear more of the arrangements coming from a bass-and-drum thing; the rhythm section's standing up. That means Edge doesn't have to play as much. On the first two albums, knowingly or not, he was covering up for a rhythm section that wasn't quite mature. We're a much tougher band now." During a playback of *War*'s "Surrender" I catch Adam's eye after hearing a particularly canny bass run. He grins wickedly: "Little something I picked up from Tina Weymouth." Like his bandmates, Adam stoked his adolescent rock fantasies with the likes of Talking

Heads, Patti Smith, and Television (The Edge clearly carries a few of Tom Verlaine's arrows in his quiver). But Adam's not unmindful of the Stones: "I was just listening to Bill Wyman last week, and he is all over the place with his bass playing, but the one thing he never tampers with is where he doesn't play, and that, I think, is the key to the Stones' sort of sloppy but rhythmic feel."

When U2 first came on the scene, "atmosphere," sooner than rhythm, was their strong point. To fill in colors the three-piece couldn't provide, Bono and The Edge sprinkled the *Boy* tracks with glockenspiel, punctuated "I Will Follow" 's bridge with the sound of breaking bottles and closed the track with a knife jammed into whirring bicycle spokes. For *October*, Edge taught himself piano, supplanting the glockenspiels, and injected searing slide guitar on "Gloria," "I Threw a Brick Through a Window," and elsewhere. (On *War*'s "Surrender" he plays a 1945 Epiphone lap steel guitar he found in Nashville.) For *War*, the band caved in the soaring cathedral they'd created with Lillywhite, stripped down to kind of "club" sound, and added violin ("Sunday Bloody Sunday" and "Drowning Man") from Stephen Wickham, whom Edge met at a Dublin bus stop. They also imported la-la's from Kid Creole's Coconuts and trumpet from Kenny Fradley. With the abandonment of that big, atmospheric sound came a greater degree of realism in the lyrics, although one cut, "Drowning Man," retains the wide-screen feel of the earlier LPs. While his bandmates went on holiday, Edge doctored the song. In a fashion similar to "bowing" a guitar, he sent his electric piano at zero volume, struck a chord, then turned it up, for a chiming, modal sound that Bono finds "Gaelic." Adam added a 6/8 bass line, and Larry, for the first time, played with brushes. Something in the song's Celtic feeling set off one of Bono's more forthright spiritual forays, and he allows as to how it may be his notion of God speaking.

"You know, 'Take my hand, I'll be here if you can—I don't want these famines to take place. These car accidents. This world of chance, this is not how I intended.' But what comes out is also a love song."

ENTRENCHMENT

This proclamation arrives simultaneously with a hard left across a narrow concrete bridge. "Bono," says Edge with the air of one used to such notifications, "the windshield wipers?" In fact, the wipers have been grinding away uselessly since a shower ended fifteen minutes ago. "This is my road," says Bono, switching them off. "On the left there, that big house belongs to Phil Lynott of Thin Lizzy. And," he says, slowing down a few yards farther along to turn into the driveway of a rather grand home, "it would appear on first notice that I have as much money as Phil Lynott. But you'll notice I'm not stopping at this house. Because I live in the stables." We jounce a few more yards to Bono's cottage on the beach, on the north side of the peninsula known as Howth Head. Tidy, with two windows glowing amber, it looks like a hard place to desert in favor of playing Indianapolis. Inside, we're greeted by Bono's wife, Alli, an apple-cheeked, dark-haired girl whose smile could be put on a tourist poster to advertise the wise sweetness of Ireland's inhabitants.

The couple were married last August, and as we head for Sutton Castle to eat dinner, they tell me about the raucous reception they held there, during which, of course, the band commandeered instruments from the hired help, climbed on a table, and assisted local folkie-turned-rocker Paul Brady with "Tutti Frutti." Bono was carried about on his brother's shoulders and spent his wedding night in the castle without benefit of electricity (which the band's exertions had snuffed). For U2 it was a celebration of more than ordinary significance—partly because it was their first work break since their Island signing in 1979, partly because Bono and Adam sealed an unspoken pact. Since the late summer of 1981, when the band came off the road to slam out *October*, Adam had grown alienated—become, in his own words, "a cynical, sometimes vicious drunk." His problems stemmed from a feeling of being sealed off from Bono, Edge, and Larry as those three grew more and more committed to their heartfelt but rather private brand of Christianity. Bono had been raised in the Church of England, a fairly austere Episcopalian flock with little resemblance to the near-charismatic worshipers he began to seek out as he entered his twenties. The Edge had similar beliefs, and Larry—especially after his mother's sudden death in a road accident—likewise became a committed Bible student. "It is what," says Bono emphatically, "gives me the strength to get up every day and put forth a hundred percent of my energy." *October* centered on Christian topics. In the depths of this estrangement—at a time when, as one insider says, "Adam may well have believed he was about to be kicked out of the band"—Bono asked Adam to be his best man at the wedding.

Adam, along with McGuinness, now supplied a hearty balance of sex, drink, and rock 'n' roll to the abstemious U2. And although he skipped out on *War*'s last sessions, when Bono was putting "40" (essentially a reading of the Fortieth Psalm) on tape, he's entirely at home with the singer's commitment. "It's very easy to be cynical about it, to knock it down. But it exists, for the public, on a heart level you can't intellectualize about, and I think Bono the singer is such an interesting person not because he stands on a street corner with his Christianity but because of the conflict within him between Christianity and the rock 'n' roll—that's what I find fascinating about him."

It was Adam who stuck around in the control booth

during Bono's tortuous *October* sessions. "I like to see Bono working under pressure, 'cause he's a great improviser, and I think he sings notes, sings words much better when he's a bit desperate. That's when the soul comes through."

The soul of the twenty-two-year-old Bono Vox is a capacious and contradictory quantity. He'll point out with some reverence that the cover of Van Morrison's *Veedon Fleece* was shot on the steps of Sutton Castle, but he is a post-punk with little reverence for rock's godfathers. He accepts the praises of Townshend, Springsteen, and Jackson Browne with none of the usual false-modest demurrers. He seems to regard the Clash as politically modish carpetbaggers ("How come the Undertones, from the trouble spot in Derry, write pop songs about their girlfriends, while the Clash, who come from an art school in London, write about Derry?") and he loathes "the whole elitist vibe" of London's fashion bands. "The whole 1976 'punk rock, man' ethic, what happened to it? The anti-star ethic, the breaking down the barrier between stage and floor, it's all out the window. They're actually saying in London, now, 'Love is in *fashion*.' That's really wild."

One reason U2 glory in their American tours is the openness, the nontrendiness, of the crowds. A quick riffle through press clippings from their last Florida sweep reveals Bono tactfully disarming a noisy kid in Tampa ("Florida does not suck. Who says Florida sucks? Are you from Florida, sir? Oh, you're from New York; I see") and jumping onstage in a Tallahassee club (after being mauled by overzealous girls at that night's show in the county Civic Center) to sing "Wild Thing" with a local band called the Slutboys. Precious Bono isn't. He didn't hesitate to walk up to future Irish Prime Minister Garret Fitzgerald in Heathrow Airport and befriend him (resulting in a Bono endorsement that was a front-page picture story in the Dublin papers). But when we pick up a girl hitchhiking to

Bellfield College, from which Bono had once been suspended, he can't bring himself to tell her he never went back because he became a rock star.

Bono says a simple grace before we dine at Sutton Castle, but it's clear that the wine does not taste like medicine to him. Before long he is giving his stage-whispered account of the Hewson family in Irish history, proceeding backward through the famine of 1840 and adducing a rather dubious blood tie to the ancient kings. Bono drops Robert Plant's name in the dust as part of an episode in a bar near the Welsh border. Plant was grabbing Adam's coat and ranting about how much he loved U2, while Bono raptly concentrated instead on a document ordering the execution of British monarch Charles I; at its foot, one of the sixteen signatures was the name MacAodha, the original Gaelic of Bono's family name, Hewson.

Bono's wife Alli looks on indulgently as he holds forth; he got his nickname not directly from the Latin for "good voice," but from the brand name of a certain hearing aid sold in the British Isles—such was the force and frequency of his palavering. The arm-swinging, stutter-stepping on-stage Bono is replaced in conversation by archings of his brow and sly grins, but the energy always shows through. His marriage, says one friend, made life easier for everyone close to him: "Here is this horny, emotional guy who also needs to live as a Christian."

Bono wrote *Boy*'s "Out of Control" immediately upon rising from a troubled sleep on his eighteenth birthday: "I said, Well, here we are. I'm eighteen, and the two most important things in my life—being born and dying—are completely out of my hands. What's the point? At that point in my life I had a lot of anger and discontent when I couldn't find answers. It was violent, but mentally violent." Thus *October*'s "I Threw a Brick Through a Window" is a kind of screed against the singer's inability to find meanings in his own life—but a brick is never mentioned except in the song's title.

From the perspective of *War*, Bono would seem to now believe he has been a bit self-indulgent. "On the first record the lyrics were impressionistic—and adolescent. On the second record, with a lot of travel behind me and a lot of experience going through the brain, I used more images—still refusing to tell the story line but giving more signposts."

ENGAGEMENT

With the band's increasing confidence, their songs, which have always borne the simple publishing credit "U2," become more truly four-sided, and their favorite metaphor of a table stabilized by four legs becomes truer. On "Seconds" (which incorporates a chant from the documentary *Soldier Girls*), Bono and The Edge sing together for the first time on record (and Adam sings his first backup vocal on "Surrender"). "Two Hearts Beat as One," Bono insists, is his try at writing a song that might get covered by Barbra Streisand or Aretha Franklin.

War's clear single is "New Year's Day." It went straight into England's Top Ten on release, and was American FM radio's most-added song the week it appeared here. Edge's guitar skitters through the verses with a special urgency, Larry's drums (recorded, to everyone's gross inconvenience, in the stone central stairway at Windmill Lane Studios) refuse to let up, and Bono gives one of his characteristically driven vocal turns. "I think we've reached the point," says Adam, "where we have the skill to direct the playing on each song right toward the feeling that caused the song to be written. We're trying to strip away everything till we get to that cause."

Much more than on the previous two albums, that

cause is to be found in a territory far afield of Bono's internal philosophical struggles—tumultuous as they may have been. It's clear he wants to strike a few pacifist blows against war's various engines—but that doesn't mean he's quit doing battle with music he finds dishonest or irrelevant to the times: "*War* is meant to be a slap in the face," says Bono, "a slap in the glossy, made-up-to-be-pretty face which is the music of most of our contemporaries."

UTOOLS

The Edge uses a Fender Stratocaster or a Gibson Explorer through a vintage Vox AC30 amp with a Memory Man echo "which is a real budget echo, but it works really well; it's functional and uncomplicated." He likes "very heavy" strings, ranging from .011 or .012 gauge up to .056. "My Explorer isn't one of the vintage '58s, it's more like a '76, but it's great in that it has a nice top end without that extra raunch and distortion that a lot of players like in a Les Paul; it's like a compromise between a Les Paul and a Strat." He admits to occasionally using a Les Paul in the studio, as well as an Epiphone steel guitar he picked up at Gruhn Guitars in Nashville. "It helps give an 'American' feel to 'Surrender,' on the new album. The Vox amps are like the original Beatle amps, with the original box speakers—little twelve-inchers with a very gutsy middle sound." The Edge is partial to Roland's Chorus 120 amps, because of their "tough, clean sound."

Bassist **Adam Clayton** favors a Fender Jazz bass played through Ampeg amps, while **Bono Vox** opts for a Shure SM-57 mike for vocals.

Larry Mullen's drum kit is a Yamaha Studio series

with Zildjian cymbals. "For 'Like a Song,' we wanted a pastoral, Celtic feel," he says, "so I got hold of a bass drum and some skins and used my hand instead of my foot."

May 1983

Up and Down and Up

with Marvin Gaye

by Nelson George

■

Marvin Gaye's words on the

phone from London were full of sadness. "There was

not the kind of love for me in Los Angeles that I was

accustomed to," he said in an eerily calm voice. "I

wanted more love, more respect for me as an artist.

There were so many plots and plans against me. People

were saying that I was finished. My personality took a

horrible beating there. I couldn't work in that kind

of psychological hellhole. I won't go back until my

tarnished image is repolished by my work. I can't do my best work in America right now."

It was the voice of a man bedeviled by events. His divorce from Anna Gordy and the cool commercial reception to *Here, My Dear* still chafed. Pressure from the IRS and other creditors had forced him to spend almost four years in self-imposed European exile. The reason for our conversation, his *In Our Lifetime* album, had been remixed by Motown, with some material deleted. Gaye still professed affection for Motown founder Berry Gordy, but he was bitter toward Motown and the whole Los Angeles music scene. To hear the man who had given such joy, from "Stubborn Kind of Fella" to "Got to Give It Up," in such personal turmoil left me feeling hollow. Marvin did add one optimistic—and prophetic—comment. He spoke of a "dark period" in his life ending and said that "perhaps now I'll experience an equal period of good fortune." I certainly hoped he was right, but I have to admit I was skeptical.

SPRING 1983

A clear blue day in San Mateo, California, part of the area known as Silicon Valley. Past Apple Computer's current building (another is going up across the street) and down the road a bit is the Villa, a nondescript motel housing Marvin Gaye for five days while he appears at a nearby concert hall. Sitting in a robe and slippers, surrounded by bodyguards and roadies, Gaye is watching a fight, quite pleased that his man is winning. ("I told you he'd walk into that right!")

Gaye appears relaxed and he has every reason to be. The IRS is off his back. He's living in the United States again, and on the strength of "Sexual Healing" is enjoying a platinum album, *Midnight Love*, and a sold-out concert tour backed by a powerful twenty-four-piece band. He even sang the national anthem at the NBA All-Star game; his performance was a hot video item on both coasts and the B-side of a single. *Midnight Love* (his first Columbia album) is virtually a one-man show, recorded in Belgium with Gaye relying heavily on synthesizers. For skeptics like me, it certified that Gaye had lost none of his musical intelligence or commercial acumen.

Yet in the midst of celebrating the biggest-selling album of his career, Gaye still seemed restless and disturbed. The battle of love versus lust that has dominated all his albums since *Let's Get It On*, the desire for lasting spiritual salvation introduced on his landmark *What's Going On*, and the personal idiosyncrasies that make his concerts an adventure still bedevil him. Despite being the most intelligently passionate pop singer of his generation, Gaye still worries over little things like his microphone technique. As he says in the following interview, "No conflicts are resolved," and for Marvin Gaye that definitely seems true.

MUSICIAN: *I've read so much about your not enjoying live performance, but you were enjoying yourself last night.*

GAYE: Well, I did, but it's sort of a mixed-emotion thing. I'm performing under stress, but it's okay, because I get a lot of positive reaction from the audience and those who love me. I can exist on that alone, but I can also pick up negative responses just as surely.

MUSICIAN: *What kind of negative things do you pick up?*

GAYE: I don't know. I feel, that's all I can say. I feel and I know my house and my crowds. I've been doing this for about twenty-five years, so it comes to a point when you can sense hostility or interest or love. I can also tell you almost how many adoring fans I have in the audience as opposed to critics and people who are there just out of curiosity. I guess I put out what I get back. I'm very honest in my performances. I'm not mechanical at all onstage. So, naturally, being a performer like that, I will have some good shows and some bad shows. I prefer it that way. I work according to how my heart feels.

MUSICIAN: *Last night you really fooled the band when you went into that medley, songs you recorded with Tammi Terrell, Mary Wells, and Diana Ross. They were looking around at each other and searching through their charts.*

GAYE: I'm not the easiest guy for a band director to work with unless we really have good rapport. McKinley Jackson has been arranging for years and he's incredible, but this is our first tour together and as we go along, he will get used to those zingers. I'm an ad-libber, you know. I love to ad-lib.

MUSICIAN: *It's amazing—you had twenty-four pieces, with three percussionists, three synthesizers, seven horns— but it all supported your voice and didn't overpower it.*

GAYE: During rehearsal we were looking at that, thinking it might be too much. I decided that we would keep the three keyboards and three percussionists because they seemed extremely compatible and I liked the sound of it. In order for a performer to be able to perform onstage and make an artistic statement, he can't save anything.

MUSICIAN: *I notice that you rearranged most of your older material. As opposed to the original version, the new "Heard It Through the Grapevine" was very slowed down.*

GAYE: There comes a time in life when you better slow down a bit. I'm forty-four years old and I'm not exactly a kid or spring chicken. This is the time to slow down a bit and take it easy, or as easy as I can, although I'm not the most unanimated act in show business. You know, I don't know how long I can keep up this sex image stuff, but I'm not going to do it much longer.

MUSICIAN: *Your frank approach to sensuality since* Let's Get It On *has certainly been influential.*

GAYE: Oh, I think my approach to sensuality and sexuality is that of subtle exhibitionist. I can't deal with the raw fact. I'd rather be teased by a woman before I get it. That's the French way: You make a person think you are going to do something, but never do until you are ready. I kind of borrowed that from the French. I actually won't be stripping down to the shorts or anything like that, though they may think I will. But that's out of the question.

MUSICIAN: *Your last album,* In Our Lifetime, *revolved around the conflicts between sex and love, sex and spirituality.* Midnight Love *is more straightforward in its view of love and sex. Has that conflict been resolved in your mind?*

GAYE: No conflicts are resolved, but I think I have taken the personal edge off it on *Midnight Love.* I tend to write of my personal interest. In this album I tend to generalize about situations. Perhaps I will go back to writing more personally on my next one.

MUSICIAN: *How long does it take you to write?*

GAYE: If it's inspired, seconds, minutes. If it's contrived, hours, days, months.

MUSICIAN: *Is there anything on* Midnight Love *that you would consider contrived?*

GAYE: A couple of songs, yes. I have to think about it a minute . . . "Midnight Lady" is one that'll give you a good example of what I mean. You're surprised I'm so honest. My honesty has gotten me in trouble in the past, but one can't be a true artist without it.

MUSICIAN: *Your old friend Harvey Fuqua played a prominent role in this album. What did he contribute?*

GAYE: I was pretty much bogged down overseas. I didn't have the technical instruments and musicians I needed and I was not about to fly back and forth to look for them. Harvey was invaluable to me in this area. He was able to go to America and supervise McKinley Jackson doing the horn arrangements and things like that.

MUSICIAN: *Throughout your career, others—Harvey Fu-*

qua on your early work, Leon Ware [I Want You], Alfred Cleveland [What's Going On] and Ed Townsend [Let's Get It On]—have written or produced your music with you. Do you feel the need for an objective pair of ears in the studio?

GAYE: Contrary to popular belief, I am quite produceable and I enjoy the role of interpreter. I love it when someone wants to produce me and I'm able to give them what they want. I think I'm going to let Barry White produce my next album.

MUSICIAN: *That's rather surprising. Some might say you would be giving Barry a big break at this stage of his career.*

GAYE: Oh, I wouldn't look at it like that. Barry White is a tremendous talent and I think I can sing Barry White's music. I think it would be a great marriage.

MUSICIAN: *The arrangements on* Midnight Love *are much cleaner than those of any of your albums since* Let's Get It On. *The vocals in particular are more defined.*

GAYE: A lot of that has to do with my microphone technique. I have a very sensitive voice. It doesn't record the same as most people's and I have to be extremely aware of my technique when I am recording. In the past I had not been perfecting my microphone technique, but while I was in Europe I studied it. I think I found what I need to make my voice more recordable.

MUSICIAN: *During your performance you twisted and turned your microphone, as I've seen some jazz singers do.*

GAYE: Well, it's because I have three voices: a very rough voice, a falsetto, and my natural and smooth midrange. Each one demands a different microphone technique. The more falsetto I sing, the closer I make the microphone, for example. This was only my fifth show, so it will take a week or so to get in shape. When I'm at that point, I won't have to deal with the microphone so much.

MUSICIAN: *It struck me that perhaps your great reliance on synthesizers on* Midnight Love *affected the writing.*

GAYE: I've been using them for a few years now. Stevie [Wonder] gave the Moog to me. I like the way I can write and produce myself with all the music coming from me. It gives me a control and feeling of self-containment that I enjoy. But one does need a change, which is why I mentioned Barry White.

MUSICIAN: *Isn't working primarily by yourself slower than working with a band?*

GAYE: Not really. That's traditionalism and I disdain tradition. I have to change totally from thing to thing or I get bored easily.

MUSICIAN: *Have you considered touring with just synths?*

GAYE: I thought about hooking it up that way and if I hadn't found the proper musicians, I probably would have.

MUSICIAN: *Since* What's Going On, *you've moved away from politics in your songwriting, though you do make mention of Bob Marley, albeit subtly, on "Third World Girl."*

GAYE: I am surprised you picked up on that. I am not about to capitalize on a man's death. I tried to refer to him indirectly out of respect. Thank you.

MUSICIAN: *The times seem to call for the kind of commentary you provided on* What's Going On.

GAYE: It seems to me that I have to do some soul-searching to see what I want to say. You can say something. Or you can say something profound. It calls for fasting, feeling, praying, lots of prayer, and maybe we can come up with a more spiritual social statement to give people more food for thought.

MUSICIAN: *I take it that this process hasn't been going on within you for quite some time.*

GAYE: I have been apathetic, because I know the end is near. Sometimes I feel like going off and taking a vacation and enjoying the last ten or fifteen years and forgetting about my message, which I feel is in a form of being a true messenger of God. I was thinking this morning that in my stage performance, I am not putting out the message like I should. Today I already decided that I am going to make a slight change.

MUSICIAN: *What about doing what Al Green did and turning your back on the whole thing?*

GAYE: That's his role. My role is not necessarily his. That doesn't make me a devil. It's just that my role is different, you see. If he wants to turn to God and become without sin and have his reputation become that, then that is what it should be. I am not concerned with what my role should be. I am only concerned with completing my mission here on earth. My mission is what it is and I think I'm presenting it in a proper way. What people think about me is their business.

MUSICIAN: *What is your mission?*

GAYE: My mission is to tell the world and the people about the upcoming holocaust and to find all of those of higher consciousness who can be saved. The rest can be left alone.

MUSICIAN: *Yet your new music deals purely with romance.*

GAYE: For legitimacy I need worldwide exposure. This is a chance for the world to recognize Marvin Gaye so that ultimately I can get my message across. If it's through romance, et cetera, then that's what it is. I have to deal with God.

MUSICIAN: *In your later years with Motown, your relationship with them was very poor. I remember in the late seventies you released a single, "Ego Tripping Out," that was later pulled from the market. It was supposed to be the lead-in to an album called* Love Man. *But your next album turned out to be called* In Our Lifetime.

GAYE: That was a single written about myself at a time when I was trying to get a handle on my ego, which was always at the forefront. I'm very self-centered and I feel like I'm it. When one is that ill, one has to try to deal with his ego. They never really gave me a chance to complete it and when I did complete it, for some reason they didn't put it on the album.

The album didn't come out the way I had done it. It's like taking a Leonardo da Vinci and submitting it to your agent and your agent has another artist paint a different smile or something on top of it. I view people tampering with my art in the same context.

MUSICIAN: *"Got to Give It Up" was released under curious circumstances. Here was almost twelve minutes of pure funk stuck onto this live package,* Live in London, *which seemed to be almost filler, an excuse to put out the long version of "Give It Up" at LP prices.*

GAYE: The reason I did that was that it was the closest I was going to get to doing disco, despite what some forces wished. I thought it was ridiculous and I refused to get into that madness. That was as close as I was coming. I just said I was going to ride out that crazy disco number.

MUSICIAN: *How much creative input did you have on the music you recorded at Motown during the Sixties?*

GAYE: In those days I probably wrote seventy-five to ninety percent of every song my name was on. As a writer in those days I was very generous and I gave a lot. If someone contributed a word or a chord, I'd give them twenty-five percent of a song, things like that.

MUSICIAN: *Did you play drums on most of your records?*

GAYE: I played drums on quite a few of my songs and also on some of Smokey Robinson's. I traveled with Smokey on the road on occasion in the early days as well. Benny Benjamin played drums on most of the songs, but if it wasn't a heavy reading thing or stuff like that, I would do it myself. Stevie played on a few things, too.

MUSICIAN: *I talked with James Jamerson, the Motown bassist, and he claims many of the production and musical ideas came from the band and not just the producers.*

GAYE: He's absolutely right. Jamerson was a genius. The little group that they had there was the Motown sound, and half the credit for the productions should go to the musicians, who were not only great musicians, but great producers and arrangers as well. They didn't get enough credit. I don't feel that's very good. It's unfortunate.

MUSICIAN: *Why did that happen?*

GAYE: Because they didn't make it happen. You give your input out of love and expect nothing or you give it and sign a contract. If you want something, you say, "I'm not giving it up until I sign something and get something for it."

MUSICIAN: *Do you listen to a lot of third-world music?*

GAYE: I have not been exposed to it here in the States, but when I was in Europe I was exposed to a tremendous amount of it. If you listen closely to my new album, it is quite evident that I was influenced by it on "Third World Girl" and "Sexual Healing."

MUSICIAN: *Did you ever get a chance to meet Bob Marley?*

GAYE: We were on tour together for three weeks in the Seventies, but I never met him face-to-face. I had tremendous respect for him. He was a great man. He was one of the greatest men in the history of the world. I view him from that perspective. I know what he had given up and I know where his heart was, so I am very sorry I never got a chance to shake his hand.

MUSICIAN: *You radically dismembered the national anthem at the NBA All-Star game. In fact, when you finished with it, it really was a different, surprisingly soulful song.*

GAYE: Thank you. . . . It's difficult to deal with the national anthem because of its structure. It was written for an operatic type of voice. A soul singer isn't exactly comfortable singing it, nor is any other ethnic person, really. So I think in a country full of ethnic nationalities, we should sing it in accordance with what is most comfortable. I can't sing it white and say I am totally white. I have to sing it so it moves *me*. Since I am a soul singer I must sing it with soul. Those who are afraid of the sound can't sing it my way and I can't see singing it their way. If I'm categorized as a soul singer, I'm going to sing like one.

MUSICIAN: *How about calling yourself a pop-soul singer?*

GAYE: I don't know what that is [*laughs*]. Unless they say that we're going to let you make it halfway, that you're going to come up here where the "big boys," the white boys, are, so you can be half-soul. You see, the pop artists are the ones who make the money, but soul artists are not supposed to make a lot of money. They are exploitable. Pop means making money. Soul means exploit.

MUSICIAN: *Some say Lionel Richie has sold his soul to make money.*

GAYE: Well, I don't know. I have a lot of respect for Lionel. . . . But if he did, I hope he got a good deal.

August 1983

PRINCE:

STRANGE TALES FROM

ANDRE'S BASEMENT...

AND OTHER

FANTASIES COME TRUE

BY BARBARA GRAUSTARK

■

Sure he's a weird kid. For Prince Rogers Nelson, a man for whom Henry Miller and Howard Hughes are undoubtedly behavioral models, the two S's of sex and secrecy are paramount. His reluctance to talk to the press is well established and his role as a beacon of sexual controversy is past legendary. Jimi Hendrix may have helped open the floodgates when he asked an innocent generation "Are you experienced?" but Prince didn't have to ask. His sexual excesses in a dank, dark Minneapolis basement with his confidant and companion Andre Cymone and a host of neighborhood girls shaped the values of his earliest songs and mirrored the experiences and insecurity of a liberated generation.

His first albums were full of funky innuendo. *For You* established him as a poetic prince of love, with a mission to spread a sexy message here on earth—a message reinforced by his "special thanks to God" credit on the LP's jacket. Prince had heard the call, all right, but it wasn't the Lord's sermon he was preaching, and with his next album, *Dirty Mind*, he catapulted out of the closet and into the public eye as a raunchy prophet of porn.

That album established Prince in rock critical circles as a truly special case. He created his own musical world in which heavy-metal guitars crashed into synth-funk rhythms and rockabilly bounced off rapid punk tempos, all of it riding under lyrical themes of incest, lost love, sexual discovery, and oral gratification. It was then that I became interested in talking to this elusive boy genius.

His concerts that fall had been a hot, erotic blast of wind through the chilly Northeast, and I was primed to meet a swaggering conqueror. What I found facing me that morning was shockingly different. Despite the studded trenchcoat, the leather jock bikini and the blatant bare chest, he was a shy and unsure man-child, a creature small as a leprechaun and just as elusive.

The interview became a lengthy excursion into Prince's pained past and through songs that had a purpose beyond the titillating of fantasies, as I was soon to learn. Prince's preoccupation, disclosed between the lines of the interview, was loneliness, which in the world had become painfully interwoven with sexuality. His own childhood was something else. Multiracial, one of nine children of a hardworking Italian mother and a half-black father—

a struggling musician who was mostly absent during his youth—Prince was a veteran of foster homes and a chronic runaway.

At the time of our interview he was proud and hurt, contemplating ending interviews altogether. He communicated with the gravity of a crestfallen child, speaking in short grudging bursts of words that nevertheless revealed a great deal more than he wanted anyone to know. At the end of our long visit he gave an eloquent summation: "That was the longest I've ever talked." He gave me an uncertain grin and as he trudged off into the New York rain, wobbling a bit on his high-heeled cobra boots, I liked him immediately and had the feeling that Prince would survive his current bout with success.

MUSICIAN: *Let me start off with* the *question, to me at least.* Dirty Mind *seems to be the antithesis of what sex should be. Or is it? Why was that album called* Dirty Mind?

PRINCE: Well, that was kind of a put-on. . . . I wanted to put it out there that way and in time show people that's *not* what sex was about. You can say a bad word over and over again and sooner or later it won't be bad anymore if everybody starts doing it.

MUSICIAN: *Are songs like "Head" and "Sister" serious or satiric?*

PRINCE: "Sister" is serious. "Head" could be taken as satire. No one's laughing when I'm saying it, so I don't know. If people get enjoyment out of it and laugh, that's fine. All the stuff on the record is true experiences and things that have occurred around me and the way I feel about things. I wasn't laughing when I did it. So I don't suppose it was intended that way.

That's why I stopped doing interviews. I started and I stopped abruptly because of that. People weren't taking me seriously and I was being misunderstood. Everything I said they didn't believe anyway. They didn't believe my name. They didn't believe anything.

MUSICIAN: *Your father's stage name was Prince Rogers. Was that his real name?*

PRINCE: That wasn't his real name. He made it up.

MUSICIAN: *And what's your last name? Is it Nelson?*

PRINCE: I don't know.

MUSICIAN: *Your point about being misunderstood is kind of important. We should try and be as straight as possible with each other so I know what you're saying is being interpreted correctly.*

PRINCE: Okay. I tell the truth about everything but my last name. I just hate it. I know how it's just the name that he had to go through life with, and he hated it, too. So that's why he gave me this name and that's why he changed his when he went onstage. I just don't like it and I just really would rather not have it out. It's just a stupid name that means nothing to my ancestry, my father, and what he was about.

MUSICIAN: *Was your father very much there when you were growing up?*

PRINCE: Well, up until the time I was seven he was very much there. Then he was very much away. Then I went to live with him once. . . . I ran away the first time when I was twelve. And then he worked two jobs. He worked a day job and then he worked downtown playing behind strippers. So he was away and I didn't see him much then, only while he was shaving or something like that. We didn't talk so much then.

MUSICIAN: *Did he have any feelings about you being a musician? Was he a supportive person?*

PRINCE: I don't think so because he didn't think I was very good. I didn't think so, either. When I finally got a band together, he used to come and watch us play every once in a while. But he finds it really hard to show emotion. I find that true of most men and it's kind of a drag, but . . .

MUSICIAN: *Is your father a good musician? What does he play?*

PRINCE: Piano. The reason he's good is that he's totally . . . He can't stand any music other than his. He doesn't listen to *anybody*. And he's really strange. He told me one time that he has dreams where he'd see a keyboard in front of his eyes and he'd see his hands on the keyboard and he'd hear a melody. And he can get up and it can be like four-thirty A.M. and he can walk right downstairs to his piano and play the melody. And to me that's amazing because there's no work involved really; he's just given a gift in each song. He never comes out of the house unless it's to get something to eat and he goes right back in and he plays all the time. His music . . . One day I hope you'll get to hear it. It's just—it sounds like nothing I've ever heard.

MUSICIAN: *How did you get into music? Where were you? What were you doing?*

PRINCE: I was at home living with my mother and my sister, and he had just gone and left his piano. He didn't allow anybody to play it when he was there because we would just bang on it. So once he left, then I started doing it because nobody else would. Everything was cool, I think, until my father left, and then it got kinda hairy. My stepdad came along when I was nine or ten and I disliked him immediately, because he dealt with a lot of materialistic things. He would bring us a lot of presents all the time, rather than sit down and talk with us and give us companionship. I got real bitter because of that, and I would say all the things that I disliked about him, rather than tell him what I really needed. Which was a mistake, and it kind of hurt our relationship.

I don't think they wanted me to be a musician, but I think it was mainly because of my father, who disliked the idea that he was a musician, and it really broke up their life. I think that's why he probably named me what he named me, it was like a blow to her—"He's gonna grow up the same way, so don't even worry about him." And that's exactly what I did.

I was about thirteen when I moved away. I didn't really realize other music until I had to. And that was when I got my own band and we had to play Top Forty songs. Anything that was a hit, didn't matter who it was. We played everything because we were playing for white and black audiences at the time. Minneapolis is mostly white anyway.

MUSICIAN: *Do you feel a strong identification with anything . . . anybody?*

PRINCE: No. I think society says if you've got a little black in you that's what you are. I don't.

MUSICIAN: *When you moved away, did you move in with your father?*

PRINCE: Well, that was when I went to live with my aunt, also in Minneapolis, because I couldn't stay at my father's. And my father wouldn't get me a piano, it was too much or whatever, so . . . he got me a guitar. I didn't learn to play the *right* way, because I tuned it to a straight A chord so it was really strange. When I first started playing guitar, I just did chords and things like that, and I didn't really get into soloing and all that until later, when I started making records. I can't think of any foremost great guitarist that stuck in my mind. It was just solos on records, and it was just dumb stuff; I hated Top Forty. Everybody in the band hated it. It was what was holding us back. And we were trying to escape it. But we had to do it to make enough money to make demo tapes.

MUSICIAN: *How'd you get to Andre Cymone's cellar?*

PRINCE: Andre Cymone's house was the last stop after going from my dad's to my aunt's, to different homes and going through just a bunch of junk. And once I got there, I had realized that I was going to have to play according to the program, and do exactly what was expected of me. And I was sixteen at the time, getting ready to turn seventeen.

MUSICIAN: *Were you still in high school?*

PRINCE: Mm-hm. And that was another problem. I wasn't doing well in school, and I was going to have to. Otherwise the people around me were going to get very upset. I could come in anytime I wanted, I could have girls spend the night, and it didn't make a difference. I think it had a great deal to do with me coming out into my own, and discovering myself. I mean, the music was interesting at that time, once I got out of high school. And I got out of high school early, when I was like sixteen.

MUSICIAN: *Did you finish?*

PRINCE: Yeah. Because I got all the required credits. And that's relatively early. In about two and a half years, or something like that. It was pretty easy and stupid. To this day, I don't use anything that they taught me. Get your jar, and dissect frogs and stuff like that.

MUSICIAN: *How'd you support yourself?*

PRINCE: Well, that was the problem. Once I got out of high school, it was interesting for a while because I didn't have any money, I didn't have any school, and I didn't have any dependents, I didn't have any kids, or girlfriends, or anything. I had cut myself off totally from everything. And that's when I really started writing. I was writing like three or four songs a day. And they were all really long. Which is interesting for me as a writer, because it's hard to just take a thought and continue it for a long period of time without losing it. And it's harder for me now to write than it was back then, because there's so many people around me now. I wrote a lot of sexual songs back then, but they were mainly things that I *wanted* to go on, not things that were going on. Which is different from what I write about now.

MUSICIAN: *You mean, what you were writing about then was just a fantasy of women?*

PRINCE: All fantasies, yeah. Because I didn't have anything around me. . . . There were no people. No anything. When I started writing, I cut myself off from relationships with women.

MUSICIAN: *Did you ever have a relationship?*

PRINCE: Several solid relationships [*laughs*]. When you're broke and poor and hungry, you usually try to find friends who are gonna help you out.

MUSICIAN: *Who are rich and things?*

PRINCE: Yeah. And successful. And have a lot of food in their fridge. I don't know.

MUSICIAN: *Did you ever do anything that you're embarrassed about?*

PRINCE: Mmm . . . no . . . well . . .

MUSICIAN: *Were you doing drugs?*

PRINCE: No. One thing that turned me off to that was seeing my brother get high. At first we all thought it was funny, but then I started asking him questions and he couldn't answer 'em, you know. So I felt it was kinda stupid. And I didn't want my mind all cloudy at any time, because I always felt . . . I don't know, maybe it was a basic paranoia or something about me, but I didn't want anybody sneaking up behind me and doing me in, or taking my money, or tricking me in any way. So I never wanted to get high.

MUSICIAN: *How does Andre Cymone fit into all of this? Was he there at the beginning, and then you went to New York and came back, and resumed the friendship?*

PRINCE: Well, what happened was, before I went to New York we lost our friendship, because he was in the band with me at the time, and I asked them all what they wanted to do, "Do you want to stay here, or do you want to go to New York?" And Andre didn't speak up, but everyone else was against it. No one wanted to do it. They liked their lifestyle, I guess. I don't think they really liked the idea of me trying to manipulate the band so much. I was always trying to get us to do something different, and I was always teamed up on for that. Like, in an argument or something like that, or a fight, or whatever . . . it was always me against them. That's when I wrote "Soft and Wet," which was the first single I put out. I really liked the tune, but everyone thought it was filthy, and "you didn't have no business doing stuff without us, anyway." I just did what I wanted to do. And that was it.

MUSICIAN: *When did you realize that?*

PRINCE: When I was in Andre's basement. I found out a lot about myself then. The only reason I stayed was because of Andre's mother. She would let me do anything I wanted to, but she said, "All I care about is you finishing school." *Anything.*

MUSICIAN: *How much can you do in a basement?*

PRINCE: Well, it depends on how many people are there! [*laughs*] You know, one time she came down and saw a lot of us down there, and we weren't all dressed, and stuff like that. It kind of tripped her out, and we got into a semi-argument, and whatever, but it was . . . you know . . .

MUSICIAN: *Was the scene back then in the basement a heterosexual scene? Was it homosexual?*

PRINCE: No, everything was heterosexual. I didn't know any homosexuals, no. There was one guy who walked around in women's clothes, but we didn't know *why* he did it, we just thought it was funny, and that was that. Some things don't dawn on you for a long time. And now I hear, like . . . Minneapolis is supposed to be like . . . the third largest gay city in the country, or whatever. Huge.

MUSICIAN: *Were you ready for New York when you came?*

PRINCE: Yeah. I was ready for anything. I felt disgusted with my life in Minneapolis.

MUSICIAN: *What'd you do when you got here? Did you know you were gonna live with your sister?*

PRINCE: Mm-hm. When I called her and told her what had happened, she said, "Well, come here and I'll help you." And I came. She had a great personality. You know, all my friends were girls, okay? I didn't have any male friends, because they were just cheap, all of 'em were just cheap, so I knew then that if she used her personality and her sensitivity, she could get us a deal. That didn't mean going to bed with anybody, it just meant that . . . you know, use your charm rather than trying to go in there and be this man, because you're *not.*

And then my sister was introduced to this one guy who had a band. And I don't know how she got this, but it was really cool. She found out everything he did, and found out that he had a demo and he was gonna take it to this woman named Danielle. And he was gonna try to get his band signed to her. So we all went together, and she said, "Can my little brother come in?" And she said sure. So we were all sitting there, and Danielle said, "All right, put your tape on." So he put on the tape of his band. That tape was pretty terrible, and Danielle said so, and the guy started making excuses, saying, "Well, that's not the real guitar player, *or* the real singers, so don't worry about it." And she said, "Well, why did you bring a tape that doesn't have the real musicians?"

Then my sister started telling Danielle about me and finally she asked me to sing. And I said no [*laughs*]. And she said, "Why not?" And I said, "Because I'm scared." And she said, "You don't have to be scared." And they turned the lights down and it was really strange.

That same day I had just written "Baby," and I didn't really have it all together, but I sang the melody and she really liked my voice. She said, "I don't care what you do, just hum, because I just want to hear you sing." So that's what I did, just started singing and humming, and making up words and really stupid stuff.

MUSICIAN: *Were you singing in your upper register then?*

PRINCE: I only sang like that back then because, I don't know . . . it hurt . . . it hurt my voice to sing in the lower register. I couldn't make it, I couldn't peak songs the way I wanted to, and things like that, so I never used it.

MUSICIAN: *Did Danielle sign you to a contract?*

PRINCE: Well, she wanted to start working with me immediately. Nevertheless, this guy was pretty upset that he didn't get his band in there. He and my sister fell out right away, but she didn't care. And that's what I dug about her. So I talked with Danielle, and she told me to come over to her apartment. She was very beautiful, too, which made everything a lot easier, I remember that about her. And she made me bring all my songs, and we went through 'em all, and she didn't like any of 'em.

MUSICIAN: *None of them? Not even "Soft and Wet"?*

PRINCE: None. Except for "Baby." She wanted me to do "Baby" with a lot of orchestration, timpani, strings, and—

MUSICIAN: *How'd that sound to you?*

PRINCE: I didn't care. You know. I was cool with it. All I wanted to do was play a couple of instruments on it, and let it say on the album that I played something. And she said no, unless I could play better than the session guy, which I didn't think I could do if a guy was gonna sit there and read the chart. I'd get aced out right away. So that didn't materialize. Anyway . . . after I finished that, that's when me and my sister kinda had a dispute.

MUSICIAN: *About what?*

PRINCE: Mainly money. I had nothing; I was running up sort of a bill there, at her place, and she wanted me to sell my publishing for like $380 or something like that—which I thought was kinda foolish. And I keep telling her that I could get my own publishing company. I didn't care about money. I just didn't care about money. And, I don't know, I never have, because ... the one time I did have it was when my stepdad lived there, and I know I was extremely bitter then.

MUSICIAN: *And did you have to go back to Minneapolis?*

PRINCE: I didn't *have* to, which was nice. Danielle knew this was gonna happen sooner or later. It was all really interesting to me back then, and I kind of would have liked to have seen what would have happened if she had managed me.

MUSICIAN: *What* did *happen? Why didn't she?*

PRINCE: Well, when I got back to Minneapolis, that's when I first met Owen Husney. I had been talking to him over the phone, and all he kept saying was that he thought I was really great, and that—

MUSICIAN: *Was Owen big-time then?*

PRINCE: He had promoted some gigs, but he was working mainly in his ad company. And he wanted to manage an act. The main thing he said was that no one should produce a record of mine—*I* should do it. I still had a deal with Danielle if I wanted it, but something about him saying that to me made me think this was the way to go. So I told her I was going to college.

MUSICIAN: *Was Danielle somebody that you had a relationship with?*

PRINCE: Mm-mm. It was only ... it was only mind games. I mean, we'd look at one another and ... play games, but it wasn't ... we never said anything.

MUSICIAN: *Um ... when you came back and started*

working with Owen, what did he do? Did he get the contract for you with Warner Brothers?

PRINCE: Owen believed in me, he really did. First of all, nobody believed I could play all the instruments.

MUSICIAN: *How many instruments do you play?*

PRINCE: Well, on the demo tapes I didn't play too many—I played drums, keyboards, bass and guitars, percussion and vocals; but when I did my album, I did tons of things. Somebody counted and said I had played twenty-seven on the first album. Different ones, but I don't know, I never count things [*laughs*]. Because the quantity is . . . people put so much emphasis on that. It's about the quantity, and what it sounds like.

MUSICIAN: *It must have been a battle with the record company to produce and arrange.*

PRINCE: Well, I got a couple offers and the only difference between Warner Brothers and the others was that they didn't want to let me do production, they didn't want to let me plan anything on the records. Warners had a lot of problems with it at first, but Owen was fighting for control for me. They made me do a demo tape. So I did it, and they said that's pretty good, do another one. So I did another one. And they called me back and they said I couldn't produce. I had to go through that process a few more times. Then finally they said okay. It was kind of frustrating at first, but I got used to it.

To some degree in the earlier days I was listening to Owen and the company. I didn't want to create any waves because I was brand-new, and stuff like that. But now I feel that I'm going to have to do exactly what's on my mind and be exactly the way I am. Otherwise sooner or later down the road I'm going to be in a corner sucking my thumb or something. I don't want to lose it. I just want to do what I'm really about.

MUSICIAN: *Did you know what you wanted to do when*

you started out? When you got that contract with Warner Brothers and they said to go into the studio and do it?

PRINCE: I had an idea, but it was really vague, and I think that had to do with . . . at least, with having such a big budget. It was really big—over a hundred thousand dollars. You're supposed to go in and do an album for sixty thousand. But I went in and kept going and kept going and kept going. I got in a lot of trouble for it.

MUSICIAN: *How much time did you spend in the studio?*

PRINCE: Hours. Hours. I was a physical wreck when I finished the record. . . . It took me five months to do the first one. I'm proud of it, in the sense that it's mistake-free, and it's perfect. And it's . . . that's the problem with it, you know. But it wasn't really me, it was like a machine. You know, I walked in, and I was sleepy all the time. I didn't really feel like recording for eighty percent of the record. But I did it anyway, because by the time I had gotten close to a hundred thousand dollars, it was like, you know, you were going to have to do something *great.* So by that time, I didn't want to make any mistakes. The relationship between me and the executive producer they assigned me was horrifying.

MUSICIAN: *Did Warner Brothers ever look as if they were just going to wash their hands of the whole thing?*

PRINCE: No, I don't think so, because I owed them too much money.

MUSICIAN: *They had to stick with you, so you could pay off.*

PRINCE: Yeah. At least three albums. And I didn't want to do anything like interviews or touring. I was being real stubborn and bullheaded, and Owen didn't realize how to get it out of me and make me stop. And, I don't know, our friendship died slowly after that. It just got strange.

MUSICIAN: *How did you get the whole act together? When did you get a band and decide to go on the road?*

122

PRINCE: Well, the band came right before I did the second album [*For You*].

MUSICIAN: *What happened when you went back to Minneapolis . . . first, after New York, and then, after you had actually recorded? Were you treated very differently? I mean, this was big-time with Warner Brothers.*

PRINCE: Yeah. The same people who told me I wasn't gonna be anything treated me with a lot more respect now. And it made me a much better person. It took a lot of bitterness out of me. Because that's all I really wanted; I didn't want the respect so much as I wanted friendship, real friendship. That's all that counts to me. And I tell my band members the same thing now. I mean, you have to learn to deal with me on an up-front level or else, you know, it's dead. I don't want people around me who don't do that.

MUSICIAN: *Has your music changed much since then?*

PRINCE: I think I change constantly, because I can hear the music changing. The other day I put my first three albums on and listened to the difference. And I know why I don't sound like that anymore. Because things that made sense to me and things that I liked then I don't like anymore. The way I played music, just the way I was in love a lot back then when I used to make those records. And love meant more to me then—but now I realize that people don't always tell you the truth, you know? I was really gullible back then. I believed in everybody around me. I believed in Owen, I believed in Warner Brothers, I believed in everybody. If someone said something good to me, I believed it.

MUSICIAN: *And it was reflected in your music?*

PRINCE: Yeah, I think so. It was . . .

MUSICIAN: *More romantic?*

PRINCE: Yeah. And I felt good when I was singing back then. The things I do now, I feel anger sometimes when I sing, and I can hear the difference. I'm screaming more

123

now than I used to. And things like that. I think it's just me. It also has to do with the instrumentation. It has nothing to do with trying to change styles or anything. Plus, I'm in a different environment; I see New York a little bit more. In my subconscious I'm influenced by the sinisterness of it, you know, the power. I hear sirens all the time, things like that. It's not like that in Minneapolis. If you ever go there, you'll see it's real laid-back, real quiet, and you have to make your own action. I think a lot of warped people come out of there. My friends. I know a lot of warped girls, okay? *Warped* to me means they see things differently than I would, I suppose. They talk a lot. They talk a lot about nothing. But I mean heavy. They get into it like you wouldn't believe. I mean, we could get into an hour-long conversation about my pants. You know, why they're so tight or something, you know what I mean?

MUSICIAN: *Well, why are they tight?*

PRINCE: I don't know [*laughs*]. I don't know. Because I want them to be. I just like the way they look.

MUSICIAN: *Did Warner Brothers flinch when you put "Head" on the third record?*

PRINCE: They flinched at just about everything [*laughs*].

MUSICIAN: *I wanted to ask you about the cover of* Dirty Mind. *How was that done?*

PRINCE: We were just fooling around, and we were jamming at the time. It was summertime, and we were having fun. And that's what I had on. But my coat was closed, so the photographer didn't know. I was with some friends and . . .

MUSICIAN: *Does everyone in Minneapolis just walk around in bikini underpants?*

PRINCE: [*laughs*] No. But, see . . . I don't know. I mean . . . once . . . I mean, if someone's got a big coat on, I mean, who knows what he has on? I mean, it was hot out. Everybody was saying, why you got that hot coat on? I'd say, I'm really not that hot [*laughs*]. And they'd say, you gotta be.

MUSICIAN: *I bet you flash.*

PRINCE: No. Not in. . . . It depends on who it is. But we were just jamming and stuff like that, and he didn't know that's what I had on. And so he was taking pictures and I happened to open my coat for one, just as a joke, you know? He said, 'Wow.' Like that. And, well, see, I used to wear that onstage.

MUSICIAN: *How'd you pick that image of yourself? Where did it come from?*

PRINCE: Well, I used to wear leotards and Danskins and stuff, because our stage show is really athletic and I wanted something comfortable. And my management said, "You have to at least start wearing underwear because—

MUSICIAN: *You weren't wearing any underwear?*

PRINCE: No. Kind of gross. So I said okay and started wearing underwear.

MUSICIAN: *What kind of friends were you hanging with?*

PRINCE: Prostitutes. Pimps. Drug dealers. Really bad people and preachers' daughters, you know? Which is strange, because they were the total opposite of their fathers.

MUSICIAN: *How did you meet them? At gigs?*

PRINCE: Yeah. I talk to people, and if they're real and sincere about what they're doing, and they don't really want anything out of me except to be my friends, then, you know, I go for that.

MUSICIAN: *The people who you were friendly with back then . . . that group . . . did they influence your style?*

PRINCE: Well, I think to some degree. They're really rebellious. They cut themselves off from the world, as I did. The band's attitude is, they don't listen to a lot of music and stuff like that. And the band is funny; the only time they'll go to see someone else is if they're going to talk about them or heckle. It's really sick. They're like critics.

MUSICIAN: *Are they all close friends?*

PRINCE: I don't know anymore. It's hard to say. When

we first started I think we were. That's how they got in the group. Some of them, I didn't find out if they could play until later.

MUSICIAN: *Are they concerned now about not being on the road? Do they feel that they'd like to be touring?*

PRINCE: Yeah. We all do. Once I stop, then I start writing again, or whatever, or start playing . . . fooling around, then I don't want to play out in public so much. I guess I write letters better than I talk, basically. I can write really good letters. And that's where the records come from. I can sit down and say exactly what I want. I don't have to worry about someone else next to me doing their job.

MUSICIAN: *It's funny, because you're a very imaginative guy. I would think for someone who draws on fantasies and wrote about dreams, fantasy would be important.*

PRINCE: Well, it is. But it's not so much when you're writing a letter. Do you know what I mean? If I were to write a letter to a friend and tell them about an experience, I wouldn't say how it made me *feel*. I would say exactly what I *did*, so that they could experience it, too, rather than the intellectual point of view. If you give them a situation maybe that you've encountered, or whatever, give them the basis of it, let them take it to the next stage, they make the picture in their own mind. I know I am happiest making records like this, making records that tell the truth and don't beat around the bush. Maybe I'm wrong for it, but I know the people at the concerts know exactly what the songs are about, sing right along, and are really into it. We have their attention. They understand, I think, and they're getting the message. I don't know. It seems real to me because . . . well, it is, because I'm saying exactly what's going on around me. I say everything exactly the way it is.

MUSICIAN: *Do you think people think that you're gay?*

PRINCE: Well, there's something about me, I know, that makes people think that. It must stem from the fact that I spent a lot of my time around women. Maybe they see things I don't.

MUSICIAN: *People always speak about a feminine sensibility as if it's something negative in a man. But it's usually very attractive for most women. Like a sensitiveness.*

PRINCE: I don't know. It's attractive for me. I mean, I would like to be a more loving person, and be able to deal with other people's problems a little bit better. Men are really closed and cold together, I think. They don't like to cry, in other words. And I think that's wrong, because that's not true.

MUSICIAN: *Is there anything that you want me to mention that we haven't talked about?*

PRINCE: Well, I don't know, it's . . . I don't want people to get the impression that sex is all I write about. Because it's not, and the reason why it's so abundant in my writing is mainly because of my age and the things that are around me. Until you can go to college or get a nine-to-five job, then there's going to be a bunch of free time around you. And free time can only be spent in certain ways. But if people don't dig my music, then stay away from it, that's all. It's not for everybody, I don't believe. I do know that there are a lot of people wanting to be themselves out there.

MUSICIAN: *Will you always try to be controversial?*

PRINCE: That's really a strange question, because if I'm that way, then I will be forever writing that way. I don't particularly think it's so controversial. I mean, when a girl can get birth control pills at age twelve, then I know she knows just about as much as I do, or at least will be there in a short time. I think people are pretty blind to it. Pretty blind to life, and taking for granted what really goes on.

MUSICIAN: *Do you think that older people don't give the twelve- and thirteen-year-olds enough credit for knowing as much as they know?*

PRINCE: I'm sure they don't. I'm absolutely sure they don't. I mean, when my mom had stuff in her room that I could sneak in and get. Books, vibrators, all kinds of things. I did it. I'm sure everybody else does. And if I can go in there and do all that, I don't see how she figures I won't know. And the way she figures I don't know is, she doesn't sit down and tell me exactly what's going on. I never got a rap like that, and I don't know how many kids do.

MUSICIAN: *I think that a lot of kids would like to feel that there's somebody who's capturing that experience for them. And I don't think anybody really has done it before.*

PRINCE: Yeah. At the same time, you're telling them about wanting to be loved or whatever . . . Accepted. In time you can tell them about contraception and things like that, which need to be said. No one else is going to say it. I know I have definite viewpoints on a lot of different things: the school system, the way the government's run, and things like that. And I'll say them, in time. And I think they'll be accepted for what they are.

MUSICIAN: *So is that really you up there onstage?*

PRINCE: What? The way I act? Oh, yeah, without a doubt.

MUSICIAN: *In other words, when you go back to Minneapolis and you go to parties, is that you?*

PRINCE: Oh, yeah. And when I'm with my friends, I'm more like that than anything. A lot of times, when I go out to clubs, if I go, I just go to observe, and I watch people. I like to watch people. The way they act and things like that.

MUSICIAN: *So what will be the first thing you do when you get back to Minneapolis?*

PRINCE: Probably take a long bath. I haven't had one in a long time. I'm scared of hotel bathtubs.

MUSICIAN: *What do you fear?*

PRINCE: They just . . . a maid could walk in and see me.

September 1983

THE PRETENDERS

CHANGE DIAPERS AND

WRESTLE DEATH TO A DRAW

BY CHARLES M. YOUNG

■

Listen to Chrissie Hynde's

speech tics and you can tell she thinks like a writer. She

gets halfway into a cliché and the Automatic Linguistic

Tedium Eraser kicks in on her disk drive and she'll X

the sucker out before it can escape her mouth and in-

duce snores in the world at large. For example: "It can

get very touchy in the studio. At times, I've completely

freaked out and all hell will . . . ya know, whatever."

Listen to Chrissie Hynde listening to speech tics and

you can tell she does not rank patience among her

priority virtues. The speech tic "man" seems to especially annoy her. When she hears it, and sometimes when she doesn't hear it, she will drop "man" into her reply, raise it one decibel, and italicize it with sarcasm so dripping it'll leave dead patches on your lawn. Chrissie Hynde shows a higher tolerance for her own speech tics. Like so many midwesterners, she lays a heavy backbeat into her conversation with "ya know" and provides extra emphasis with "you know." For example: "It's like getting up there and just taking a chance, plunging into the deep end. Ya know, going in headfirst. Ya know, going crazy. Ya know, anarchy. So okay, let me drag my empty sack of a body, ya know, up onstage in front of three hundred thousand people [at the US Festival] with two guys I've never played with before. Ya know, let it be filmed and like the cameras are right in my face and I know I'm going to be on television, ya know, but at least I'll have a go because at the end of the day, it's just rock 'n' roll. You know. And there shouldn't be anything you're trying to prove or protect or do you know what I mean?"

II

In the past couple of years, Chrissie Hynde got pregnant, she fired her bass player, her guitar player died, her ex-bass player died, she put a new band together, she had a hit single ("Back on the Chain Gang"), she had a baby, she played the US Festival, she recorded a new album (*Learning to Crawl*), she's about to tour the world for nine months with a small baby, and a lot of journalists have been poking around probing her speech tics.

"*You* would probably say that's a pretty heavy load of stress," says Chrissie Hynde in her dressing room at London Weekend Television for a taping of "2000 Miles," the

English single. "But it's all relative. There's not a war going on or anything."

Only when compared with taking a cruise missile in the kidneys is that not an extremely heavy load of stress.

"Well, what about the girl who's twenty-five years old and still living with her parents in the suburbs?" says Hynde. Akron, Ohio, remains the dominant force in her accent after ten years in England, and it is only through sheer force of will that she manages to avoid absurdity when uttering words like *quid*.

"Maybe she's working in the health food store part-time, or maybe she's not working at all 'cause she doesn't have to. She goes to the mall two or three times a week, wanders around, has lunch at Stouffers, picks through the designer clothes at Halley Brothers, goes back home, and watches the telly. To me, a life like that would be much more mentally harrowing. And there's little motivation to get out because physically it's pretty comfortable. And the longer you stay, the harder it is to motivate because you lose that desperate desire to get out that you have when you're young. All I'm saying is, I think I've had it damned easy, not half as bad as what Sue Ellen [of "Dallas"] is going through."

So she's led this uninsulated life. . . .

"Of course, I left America to escape that insulation," says Hynde, dressed in black and white with white skin in a white room under a fluorescent light. The only thing happening visually for light-years around is her dark eyes under her dark bangs which in real life, as opposed to her photographs, she occasionally brushes out of her eyes. "And for a very physical reason: You're always in a car there. If you want to go for a walk, quite often you're the only one on the street surrounded by fifteen thousand people in cars. It made me feel like a Martian or something.

Here in London I can walk to the solicitor, to the doctor, to anyone I want to see. I swore blind I'd never own a car. And then I bought one last year. Almost for the hell of it. And I had this kid to take care of. I had a few flimsy excuses. It's in the car pound now. I don't care if they keep it."

One of those musicians who won't talk about songs because they ought to be self-explanatory nor her private life because that's nobody's business, Hynde seems a good candidate to talk some more about cars.

"You aren't going to print *that*, are you?"

She wants to go off the record about what kind of car she owns?

"Well, I think it's personal."

Okay.

"It's a [*brand name withheld by request*]."

That's not a disgusting car.

"It's a little [*brand name withheld by request*]. It's the littlest [*brand name withheld by request*] that they make. People identify so much with their cars that it's embarrassing. I just went to the lot with my girlfriend and said 'What's the cheapest car you've got?' and took it."

Born September 7, 1951—exactly fifteen years after Buddy Holly's birth and twenty-seven years before Keith Moon's death—Hynde is more willing to talk about why she is alive and many of her peers are not.

"Maybe I'm more intelligent than people who do themselves in," she says. "Maybe they're not aware of death. Maybe they don't realize they could kill themselves by accident. To me, going that quickly is horrible. I don't want to get shot in the back of the head. I'd rather someone say, 'You've got cancer and you're going to die in two months.' Most people would rather get shot in the head. I know 'cause I ask people a lot, 'What would be your least favorite way of dying?' Usually they don't even want to talk about it. 'Well, come on! What's it gonna be? A plane crash?' "

Hynde shifts moods abruptly. "This must sound terrible, making jokes. I lost two of the closest people in my life. These were people I loved. But I do think about death *all* the time. Not like I'm afraid of her, but as a reality that we're here only so long. At least with cancer you have to prepare yourself. That's why I think it's damned sloppy to overdose on drugs by accident and go to sleep and not wake up again. Your spirit can become very confused, not knowing what hit you."

III

Amid an explosion of Air Force recruiting posters ("Under the shadow of their wings, our land shall dwell secure") in manager Dave Hill's office, drummer Martin Chambers picks up a pencil holder.

"My wife has said to me several times, 'That's moved. That's gone *bonk* like that," says Chambers, moving the pencil holder a foot or so across the desk. "But I was never one to believe in anything unless I saw it myself. Then for the first time about a month ago . . . we'd just finished the album and I was feeling a bit down. I was sitting there watching television and I could see this carton of milk I'd put on the kitchen table, just as firmly as that's there." He taps the pencil holder. "Absolutely no question it's not going anywhere. It's a heavy object. No wind. No draft. No way." Chambers lifts the pencil holder and walks it to the center of the floor beyond the desk. "It went at least a yard and a half in the air and dropped to the floor. If it had fallen—and there was no way it fell—it would have landed at the edge of the table, not here.

"I just sat there glowing, feeling really pleased with myself. It was Jimmy. It was his birthday and we didn't know and we missed him. He was there. Poof."

Jimmy, James Honeyman-Scott, the late guitarist of the

135

Pretenders, grew up with a deep love for the Beach Boys and a part-time job at the local music store where he sold drumsticks to Chambers. The place was Hereford (pronounced Airyferd), located between England and Wales, populated with furrowed farmers who spend much of their time trying to talk bartenders into giving them free drinks. "They would make great music business managers," says Chambers, who dresses like a gentleman farmer himself. "They don't give a ha'penny away. They'd make Miles Copeland pay through the nose."

Not much excitement, though, for a lad with more mischief in his grin than any ten boys should be allowed, so Honeyman-Scott turned to his own devices: humor, guitars, and drugs. The humor was in the Marx Brothers tradition—charming, nonsensical, and an important ingredient toward keeping the band together during the early tours. The guitars he collected by the dozens, and his favorite pastime was talking shop with other guitarists, just about all of whom he would invite onstage for the Pretenders' encores. The drugs stopped his heart on June 16, 1982, at the age of twenty-five.

"The doctors told him, 'If you don't stop drinking, you'll kill yourself,' which was bad in a way because he did too much coke then," says Chambers. "Instead of drinking five or six pints, he would do a gram a night. Cocaine will kill and his body just said, 'Sorry, pack it up.' Thank God he was asleep. Better than walking down the street and collapsing and knowing you're going to die and having people stare at you. At least he was asleep and probably dreaming of the Great Fender in the sky."

Pete Farndon—bassist, Herefordian, and cofounder, with Hynde, of the Pretenders—had been fired from the band two days before for, oddly enough, drug abuse. Farndon's problem was smack, however, and six months later he, too, died of an overdose. Something had turned him bitter over the years—perhaps a broken love affair with Hynde at the beginning of the band, perhaps just resentment at having a woman tell him when he was too loud. He had apparently alienated most of his friends by the time of his death, but Chambers recalls him as a "great gentleman" for his gracious manners and being tragically close to putting his career back together with another band.

"I miss those blokes so bad it's unbelievable," says Chambers, his eyes asparkle with barely contained tears. "The great thing was, we were all from the same part of the country, and we all had the same humor. A lot of the best bands in history have been started by mates. If you look at those early pictures of the Beatles, you can see they're having a scream with each other. That's what it's about. When you start off, you just want to show off a bit and pull the women. But as it develops, you get to see the world with your mates."

Chambers is proud to have recently quit a two-pack-per-day habit, fishes in his spare time to keep his sanity, plans to avoid his traditional role as psychoanalyst to the road crew on the upcoming tour, and is awaiting the birth of his first child with his wife Tracy Atkinson, former secretary to the band. He finds his instrument unsubtle musically, avoids rehearsing as much as possible, and beats his drums to death when he does play. ("It's either them or me, and it won't be me.") His first effort as a songwriter has been released as the B-side to "2000 Miles" in England. It's called "Fast or Slow, the Law's the Law," a catchy and upbeat number memorializing a line from an old British movie comedy (*Ask a Policeman*) that he and Jimmy loved.

"I'll tell you another thing that was very strange," says Chambers. "After Jim had been buried, Tracy and I slipped away from the wake and went back to the grave to be alone.

We heard a school bus pull up and this kid got off. He came running into the cemetery, and he was exactly like a kid I knew in 1968 named James Honeyman-Scott. The same nose, the same straight blond hair, the same black jacket. When I first knew Jim, he was still in school in his first pair of long trousers, and this kid was the spitting image. As he came running in, full of beans, and said, 'Oh, buried 'im, 'ave they?' I said yeah. He came over and looked about. 'That's it, then, right?' And he left. No regard for formality. I felt like saying, 'Don't take up the guitar, pal. Leave it alone.' But it was a very sad day, and he'd made me laugh. It was Jim again somehow."

IV

Chrissie Hynde is credited in some quarters with being the first "punk chick." She'd as soon leave that laurel off of her résumé. It is nonetheless a fact that when she first arrived in London in 1973, seeking fame and fortune and rock 'n' roll, she terrorized the reserved English with her brashness, honesty, and binges. She hung out in the early punk scene, worked as a clerk in Malcolm McLaren's boutique Sex, took part in some of McLaren's pre-Pistol projects (the regrettably short-lived Masters of the Backside), was friends with Sid Vicious, and credits Nancy Spungen with bolloxing up the first-generation scene by bringing heroin with her from the United States. A few years older than the average punk, Hynde never rejected her more melodic influences from the Sixties and worked at refining her voice through several bands that didn't last. By the time she and the three Herefordians coalesced into the Pretenders in 1978, she had little in common with the punks other than being irritated by everything.

Their first album, *Pretenders*, was the surprise success of 1979. Hynde quavered, moaned, belted, crooned, breathed, seduced, shouted, and hit all the right notes in a combination that sounded wonderfully new and original but within all the right traditions. (She could also swear better than anyone in the history of recorded music. Check out the line "But not me, baby, I'm too precious/ So fuck off"—the sibilance in the extended f carries her right through to the k with hardly any u, setting up a thrilling epiglottal syllable division that explodes into the final f sibilance. Fearful symmetry, as they call it.) The album also revealed James Honeyman-Scott as a guitar hero of the first order, if overshadowed by Hynde. The guy was almost too versatile for his own good. He could soar with Eddie Van Halen, get low down with T-Rex, slop and throb with Keith Richards, jangle with the Searchers, and what else is there? (Well, there is "widdly-woo," Honeyman-Scott's term for long masturbatory solos. He didn't do any of them.) And the rhythm section of Martin Chambers and Pete Farndon took some truly eccentric riffs and time signatures (7/4 on "Tattooed Love Boys," 5/4 on "The Phone Call") and made them flow like a runaway raft on the Colorado.

The Pretenders had something for everyone. Critics explicated Hynde's profanity. Musicologists ate the weird time signatures off a stick (Hynde didn't even know she'd written them until Chambers counted out the songs). FM programmers hooked millions of listeners on the unforgettable melodies. Rock 'n' roll fans thanked God it wasn't more disco crap. Concertgoers could watch Hynde glare from under her bangs, Honeyman-Scott be cute and animated, Farndon be distant and handsome, and Chambers pour water on his floor toms, causing a rainbow splash into the colored lights every time he played a fill.

Most of all, journalists loved Chrissie Hynde. The woman was a walking quote machine. "For every act of sodomy I was forced to perform [while hitchhiking], I got

139

ten thousand [British] pounds to show for it now," she told Kurt Loder in *Rolling Stone*. With a little courage from the bottle, she would attack customs officials, assault cops, kick her manager in the balls. It was the stuff of legends.

"I'm just Chrissie Hynde from Akron, Ohio, ex-cocktail waitress," she now says. "I'm a female Bobo Belinsky. Remember Bobo Belinsky sitting in his armchair? He was my favorite R. Crumb cartoon. It was twelve frames and each one showed him doing nothing from a different angle. One from the ceiling. One from behind his head. One from his boots. And the caption was, 'Believe me, he's no big deal.' That's me. Not some mythical rock 'n' roll goddess."

An EP, *Extended Play*, followed in 1981 and was criticized by previously ga-ga reviewers for not being an album. When the album *Pretenders II* arrived later the same year, it was criticized for not being *Pretenders I*. Play both records back to back in 1984 and they sound almost equally good. *Pretenders II* wasn't a revelation, but what band has ever produced two revelations in a row? It had as many good songs as the first album, maybe more. Listen to "Message of Love" again and see if the phrase "like Brigitte Bardot" doesn't make you feel happy for a week. Or, if you want to feel rotten for a week, identify with the subject of "Pack It Up": "And furthermore, I don't like your trousers/ or your taste in women/ And what about your mind/ And your insipid record collection." *No* one else can sing like that.

"I don't see me as so original," says Hynde. "If I gave you all the albums I'd listened to for the last fifteen years, it would be pretty damned obvious. It's very derivative, anything that a kid sitting in Akron, Ohio, with a transistor radio could pick up on."

Yeah, well, Loverboy is a product of those influences, too, and . . .

"I don't know who that is."

They're boring.

"Then why should I listen to them?"

Everybody's a product of their influences. . . .

"My influences were probably hipper than Loverboy's. I saw Sam the Sham and the Pharaohs onstage. I saw Jackie Wilson. I saw the Yardbirds. I saw the Rolling Stones with Brian Jones. I saw Dennis Wilson throw his drumsticks in the air and storm offstage in disgust. I saw Mitch Ryder and the Detroit Wheels have a fistfight onstage. I was fourteen and it freaked me out, so I stayed around for the second show and they had the same fistfight again and I realized they had faked the whole thing. How could I possibly go wrong with influences like that?"

Ten thousand clone bands had those influences, too.

"Well, you have to learn how to sing, don't you? When I was sitting in Cleveland, starting to sing with a band, I'd go in the closet when everyone else left for their jobs and sing at the top of my lungs just to hear what the possibilities were. You can sit in an audience for years and imagine how you might sing, but you don't know until you try. One of the hard things to get over for a lot of people is learning to appreciate their own strong points. Like a girl with a weak chin always admires a girl with a big boxy chin. You always admire what you don't have. I could imitate Janis Joplin, but I sure didn't know what I had. The thing to do is just accept what you're best at. Don't try to do what you like in someone else unless it comes natural to you."

Was there a point where she came to admire what she had in herself?

"No."

She still doesn't admire what she has?

"No, I just try to do what comes naturally to me."

v

Robbie McIntosh is the Pretenders' new guitarist. He used to play with the Foster Brothers, Chris Thompson (once of Manfred Mann) and the Islands, Night (their "Hot Summer Nights" got to Number Seventeen in the States) and Dean Martin's Dog. He joined the Pretenders at the behest of his friend Honeyman-Scott, who in yet another odd coincidence called the night before he died to say the band needed another musician for the stage show and would McIntosh be interested?

"It was weird joining a band that was already successful," he says. "I didn't feel I should copy anything that Jimmy did, but his playing is such a part of the songs that it's unavoidable. People ask if I feel silly doing it, but not at all. I think it's sort of a tribute. And of course I have the new material for myself."

Most memorable McIntosh quote, upon hearing Hynde repeat Ozzy Ozbourne's remark that biting the head off a bat was like eating a Crunchie (an English candy bar) through a chamois: "I know just what he means. I ate a Crunchie through a chamois the other day, and it tasted just like the head of a bat."

Malcolm Foster is the Pretenders' new bassist. He knows McIntosh from when they went to the same high school and when they played together in the Foster Brothers, led by Malcolm's older brother Graham. He used to play rugby and remains a muscular chap through karate and judo. He is grateful to have been laid off his job as a construction estimator or he might not now be a Pretender. The Rosencrantz and Guildenstern of this play, he will be the only band member on the upcoming tour without a small baby (McIntosh's wife, like Chambers's, is pregnant). "I'll find solace somewhere," he promises.

Most memorable Foster quote: "I'd read all those things about the wild lady of rock 'n' roll. When I met her, she was already pregnant and I think that changed her a lot. I don't think there's much of the old Chrissie Hynde, the terror, left."

The sort-of fifth Pretender is Chris Thomas, who has produced all their work except the Nick Lowe–produced first single, "Stop Your Sobbing." Only McIntosh has any extensive experience working with another producer, Richard Perry.

"They're both top-class producers," says McIntosh. "But Perry is much less personable. He sort of shows up with his chauffeur and sits there and says, 'Make that sound different.' I never got to know him as a person. Chris is much more hardworking. He really knows the studio and spends a lot of time pushing buttons and moving micro- phones. Chris is so un-big-time, it's ridiculous. Chrissie takes the piss out of him if he just wears a leather jacket."

"I don't know how other people work," says Hynde, "but we have a very straightforward, methodical, obvious way of working. We go in and put down the backing track. We'll do five or six if we have to, then we'll sit down and listen to them and decide that number four and number six are best because of the great drumfill on six. Then we'll do an edit. Then we mend anything that needs it. Then we'll put in the guitar solos. When there's enough for me to work with, I'll do the vocal. I might leave it to the very end, or I might do it early on so the rest of the band can work around it. Whatever's going on, everybody's gotta be there. You can't say, 'Well, I've done my bass line. See you next Thursday when we do the next track.' That would be unheard-of in the Pretenders. If someone has a suggestion at any point, we want to hear it. That's why the album is very much a band product at the end."

The new band product, the third Pretenders album, the first with the new lineup, is *Learning to Crawl*. Themati- cally, most of the record is about pain: the vengeful pain in relationships ("I Hurt You," "Thin Line"), the nostalgic pain of loss ("My City Was Gone"), the contemptuous pain of knowing an asshole ("Time the Avenger"), and the nightmare pain of watching life crush a friend ("Back on the Chain Gang"). It's about getting out there and mixing it up with the world ("Middle of the Road"). It's about the unstoppable Sherman tank called maternal love ("Thumbelina," "Show Me"). And finally it's about washing clothes on Saturday night when everyone else is having fun ("Watching Clothes").

Musically, *Learning to Crawl* sounds remarkably like the old Pretenders. McIntosh has many of the same influences as Honeyman-Scott and seems equally at home with straight-ahead rock 'n' roll, R&B, or even the early Johnny Cash riffs in "Thumbelina." The band's reason to exist has always been Hynde's songwriting, of course, and that has remained constant.

"I'll just come in with the basic chords and the lyrics— not even that sometimes—and say, 'More of this, more of that,' " says Hynde of her creative process. "Okay, it starts out with the bass: buh duh dunt don. And then the drums: dah duh dah buh duh duh dah. And then the bass again: duh duh dump duh duh dum ding ding chingk. Duh duh dah dum duh dah dah. Dododododododododooooooooo-dunt. And then the guitar: dah duh duh day. Bass again: dunt dunt dunt. I don't know why we even bother to play instruments. I'll just stand there like a loony and sing all the parts."

How would that process translate into something like the new single, "Middle of the Road"?

"Well, it's very basic chords, isn't it?" says Hynde. "It's almost like a regular R&B song. It's like taking a basic format, like the blues, and just giving it new lyrics. . . . The Stones could never get me for plagiarism, 'cause they've been the worst at that. But you know the song 'Empty Heart' that they used to do? Well, to me this song is the same meat, different gravy. Because I used to play that song with the band and after we'd been doing 'Middle of the Road' for a while, I realized it was the same chords. So it's a very standard format. And there's not much of a melody to it. It does have a nifty guitar solo. It's just me sort of trying to sing rock 'n' roll."

VI

Peggy Sue Fender Honeyman-Scott met James Honeyman-Scott backstage at the Armadillo World Headquarters on April 10, 1980. It was her third day back in Austin after a couple of years in California, where she'd been going to college and modeling. She thought he was strange, particularly when a local journalist wanted to know if they were an item. Honeyman-Scott replied that they were engaged to be married, this after knowing her all of a few minutes. It seemed to be one joke among many that night, but he would say later that somehow he did know they would be married. And they were, exactly a year later.

"He didn't do a lot of drugs," says Peggy Sue from her boutique, Dressed to Kill, in Dallas. "Everyone goes through a phase like that. He was no worse than anybody else. He was just born with a weak liver. It's just so unfair. So unfair. After a couple of beers, he would turn yellow. Not so you'd notice, but I did, because I was with him all the time. I'd go on tour with him just to help to keep him off drink. You know how the English drink. He loved that 'mate' thing, having a pint with his friends, and it was terribly frustrating to him not to be able to do it."

After much soul-searching, she chose the following for his gravestone: "Put love into this world, and heaven with all its beatitudes and all its glory becomes a reality. Love is everything. It is the key to life, and its influences are those that move the world."

"That was Jimmy," says Peggy Sue. "He put so much love into the world. I also had a Firebird 7 engraved on the stone. It was the one guitar he still wanted and didn't have. It was my final present to him."

Did she know Martin Chambers had apparently experienced a visitation on Jimmy's birthday?

"No, I haven't talked with Martin for a while. It's difficult for me to see him because they were so similar. But that would be just like Jimmy, throwing a little tantrum because nobody was paying attention to him on his birthday."

Had she any similar experiences?

Peggy Sue pauses for a deep breath. "I don't know if I should tell you this. People will think I'm nuts. But, okay. I was sitting in my living room with my girlfriend one night about a month after he died. I walked into the bathroom and in the hall I suddenly felt someone behind me. I turned around and looked down for some reason. His feet were there. Not physically, but spirit feet somehow. It sounds weird, but I loved his feet. They were really cute feet. Then I went to the bathroom and thought, 'Oh, my God, he's watching.'

"For months afterward, I would scream and cry and tell him, or God, how much I missed him. Then one night I couldn't bear it any longer. My heart was burned out. I begged him to put me to sleep. I asked him to knock me out, and the next thing I knew it was morning. That sounds crazy, but unless you've experienced it, you don't know. But I knew it was him. And he's with me now." Peggy Sue stops for a beat. "Can you hear that over the phone? The Pretenders just came on the radio."

Chrissie Hynde stuffs a forkful of mixed vegetables into her mouth (she hasn't eaten meat for years) in the cafeteria of Radio Television Belgium, where she is awaiting yet another lip-synch taping of "2000 Miles." "You wanted to know before if I missed America, right?" she asks, sticking out her tongue with the wad of half-chewed vegetables, drawing groans from several grossed-out Europeans in the vicinity. "How can I miss America when I am America?"

Well satisfied with herself, Hynde decides to expostulate on the current state of music. "I think next year is going to be the year of the song. I've been hearing a lot of riffs lately, but no great songs. Know what I mean? We've made some great records, but I haven't written any really complete, great songs. They'll have to start writing songs again, just so Dean Martin can cover some material other than 'Something.' We gotta give the old folks some new songs. I was gonna write a letter to Frank Sinatra with a list of Kinks songs he ought to cover."

Hynde launches into an enthusiastic Sinatra-interpretation of "Sunny Afternoon," "Don't Ever Change," and "When I Go to Sleep."

"*Frank Sings Ray.* Be a great album, huh? Ray actually wrote a song for Sinatra once: 'Thanks but no thanks/ Just call me Frank/ 'Cause I mean what I say.' But that's as far as he got. I hope he finishes it."

Exactly what Hynde's relationship is to Ray Davies, leader of the Kinks, has been a matter of much speculation over the years. He is the father of their baby [*brand name withheld by request*] but is not her husband. Reading past interviews with both, one would think they sit around reinforcing each other's depression.

"I was depressed before I met Ray."

But Ray doesn't seem able to believe anything good about himself after twenty years as a rock 'n' roll star.

"Yeah. Ray is *really* depressed."

So does the baby have your personality or Ray's?

"This is it. She was born with her *own* personality. She's as happy as a lark, for a start, so she's got nothing to do with either of us."

Ray does his fair share of taking care of her?

"Hmmmmmmmmm."

You do most of the diaper changing?

"Oh, yeah."

Is he thrilled with the baby as you are?

"He loves her. Well, she is a pretty neat kid. And I have to love her. I can't take her back now, can I? If I didn't like her, I'd really be in the shit." Hynde fishes through her handbag for a snapshot of a beautiful, grinning baby. "How can you not be thrilled to see that thing? I want her to grow up to be Bobo Belinsky, too."

PRETENDER EXTENDERS

Chrissie Hynde plays a Fender Telecaster through a Fender Twin. "All I know is switching it on and off and whether it's too loud," she says. "That comes from the days when, if I was turning it up, the guy guitarist would come over and do it for me, just because he was the guy, and I would do something else. As a result, my guitar sounds like shit much of the time."

Robbie McIntosh is also a Fender fan, playing his Telecaster and Stratocaster through a new Marshall "modified by a guy named Pete Cornish to sound like an old Marshall." He has tried other pickups but always returns to the originals. "If it isn't Fender, it doesn't jangle enough."

Malcolm Foster plays a bass custom-made by Roger Griffin with parametric controls ("like having the amp controls on your guitar"). His amp is Ampeg, his strings are Guild, and he has an abalone-shell goat inlaid in the neck in honor of his astrology sign Capricorn.

Martin Chambers, one of the heaviest hitters around, just got a new drumkit from Sonor. "They're a German company, so you play them once and you feel like you're invading Poland," he explains. "You can beat hell out of them and they'll stand up to it. They're going to be completely white, even the cymbals and fittings, so it looks like one big molded piece of plastic, like the world in 1984."

March 1984

THIS IS THE REAL STORY

OF JOHNNY ROTTEN

BY CHARLES

M. YOUNG

■

What is your business in

Britain?" the customs officer wanted to know.

"I'm going to interview Johnny Rotten," I said.

"Oh," he smiled. "That will be fun."

"No," I said. "It won't."

"Really?" he said. "I always thought it was an act

he put on rather than a character defect."

"That's not an either/or proposition," I should have

said. As it was, I opted for character defect.

"Well," he said, "I saw him come through here once

on his way to America. He was traveling with his mother. I thought it was rather sweet."

According to the most recent surveys, 38.6 percent of the people who read this magazine are hosebags who write letters to the editor that say shit like, "Why don't you guys live up to the name of your magazine and use that space for a real musician like Phil Lesh/Rick Wakeman/Al DiMeola?" Under normal circumstances, I pay no attention to hosebags, don't even open their letters because I can smell hosebag attitude right through the envelope. But this article is not normal circumstances. This article is Johnny Rotten. And this one time, I gotta sympathize with you 38.6 percent hosebags: I also get unglued when I'm reminded that this Rotten dude exists on the same planet. So go ahead and send your drooling, stupid letters and know that I ache for you as I ache for King Canute commanding the tide to roll back.

'Cause, see, the difference between you hosebags and myself is that you hosebags think Rotten shouldn't be in the magazine 'cause he has no talent. I say he shouldn't be in the magazine because when I see his name in print, I am reminded that on five of the seven occasions when I met him since 1977, he came within a hair of giving me a nervous breakdown. . . . Yeah, yeah, I know: Tough job I have, flying around the world interviewing rich and famous people. But the next two years are gonna be tough on me and on all you hosebags. The Sex Pistols are coming back. A docudrama (apparently) centered on Sid Vicious and Nancy Spungen is due out. It's directed by Alex Cox, who did *Repo Man*, the best fictional treatment of punk on film ever. *The Great Rock & Roll Swindle*, the Sex Pistols' own sort of autobiographical movie, is finally going to get released in the States. And there are a number of books in the works, not the least of which I'm hoping will be my own *Blowin' Chunks: Punk Passage and Beyond* (Doubleday/

154

Dolphin), a skewed social history of punk in which the Pistols figure heavily. And then there is the matter of Rotten's own new *Album* (*Cassette* in cassette, *Single* in single), which to universal surprise is listenable and interesting and—if his reputation with radio programmers doesn't sink him again—somewhat commercial.

Let us furthermore recall why the guy is important aesthetically and historically: He changed singing. No one sounded like him before him, and thousands have tried to sound like him since him. No band has ever declared itself to the world with such force and rage as when Johnny Rotten announced he was the anti-Christ on the Sex Pistols' first single, "Anarchy in the U.K." No band did more to spawn the still-flourishing punk subculture than the Sex Pistols. Although it never broke the *Billboard* Hot 100 and radio programmers still loathe it, *Never Mind the Bollocks* remains one of the most influential albums of the Seventies, maybe *the* most influential if you count punk influence in other art forms.

And let me recall last summer, when I met Rotten in a Los Angeles saloon to get some information for my book. In two hours, the guy drinks ten screwdrivers, several of which are doubles, and, having asked every question I can think of, I figure I better get him home before he pulls his usual Jekyll and Hyde. He, however, wants sushi.

"I answered *all* your questions," he snarls.

Maybe food will sober him up, I'm figuring as I drive to Sushi on Sunset, where he eats about two grams of fish and pours down six or seven twenty-one-ounce Sapporos, growing ever more belligerent over a question I'd asked hours before. See, certain types of punks are homophobic and, like all Americans, they love to believe their heroes are homosexuals. I asked Rotten about certain rumors concerning him, which he denied (he's had a girlfriend for years), saying what difference did it make anyway? Fair enough, but as he gets drunker, he wants to deny it some more, getting increasingly irritated with me for asking in the first place, and flirting with all these women at the sushi bar to show how heterosexual he is. And he's getting louder and *louder*, really stinking out the joint for anyone interested in eating, and he's ordering numerous Sapporos for all the women he's trying to flirt with *on my tab*. I'm tellin' ya, I was hoping for botulism in my tuna roll, or maybe in his tuna roll. Course, the bastard wouldn't have eaten it anyway.

So finally he stands on the bar and announces—nay, screams—to the entire restaurant: "NO ONE EVER STUCK THEIR WILLIE UP MY BUM!!!"

Then he totters off to take a leak. This woman he's been putting the moves on—she's got dyed-black spikey hair and is wearing a Rodeo Drive designer punk outfit in black and Day-Glo pink and has a skeleton earring—leans over and asks, "Who is that guy?"

"John Lydon," I say.

"Who's that?" she asks.

"Johnny Rotten."

"Who's that?"

"He sang for the Sex Pistols. . . . You never heard of the Sex Pistols?"

"No."

Young people today, they got no respect for tradition. They don't deserve to know who this John Lydon/Johnny Rotten of the Sex Pistols/Public Image, Ltd., is. Fuck 'em. On the other hand, I want lots of young people to give me their money when my book comes out, so I'll lay out a portion of my stuff.

First of all, Johnny Rotten is one of the least informative interviews this side of politics. Interviewers tend not to notice they are getting nothing, because he is such a difficult personality that they are overly grateful or overly re-

156

sentful of any small tidbit he tosses their way. I plead guilty on both counts.

His first impulse is not to reveal but to calculate how much to reveal and/or provoke. He almost never volunteers information if you bring up a general subject in hopes that he'll ramble for a while and drop a few factoids on you. He rarely tells anecdotes, mostly just throws thunderbolts of judgment.

One of the tricks of interviewing is to shut up for a moment and let the interviewee rush to fill up the silence. Try it sometime: Conversation abhors a vacuum, and people will say *anything* to fill up those uncomfortable pauses. Rotten is the only person I ever interviewed (excluding a couple of lawyers) who is smart and sadistic enough not to fill up those silences. He loves to look haughty as I squirm and stutter to formulate the next question out of the absolute minimum of information he has revealed.

There is also the problem of what to do with one's eyes when talking to Rotten. To return his glare is to be blasted with two laser beams of contempt; it is to know you are in the presence of someone who is quite sure you are ridiculous. If you look elsewhere on his face, you are confronted with massive, deep, red, poisonous zits, the sort you could squeeze until you cry and still never pop the rot infection. His scalp is piled with hairballs so vile they would get any stray dog euthanized immediately as a public health hazard. And his body, these days, is bloated.

The biggest problem, however, is figuring out when he is telling the truth. The first insight I had into the guy's character came in 1977 when I was interviewing Sid Vicious for a cover story on the Pistols. Vicious had attended Kingsbury College (a "college of further education," which is the equivalent of American high school) and recalled that John had once skipped school and returned with the excuse that he had piles so long they were hanging out his

157

pants and he had to cut them off with a razor. The teachers had *believed* him, even sent him flowers. Rotten confirmed the story in 1977 (describing himself as an "atrocious liar") and again in 1986. Like any good politician, he learned early that the most outrageously absurd lie, if propounded with enough emotional force, will be believed. At the same time, his life has been so strange that you cannot dismiss anything out of hand. One of the early stories about Rotten was that he once had a job as a rat killer in a cesspool. To the extent the story has been repeated, it has been assumed to be part of the Sex Pistols' hype, a lie calculated to build their legend. But he really was a rat killer in a cesspool.

"He used to work with me in the crane when he was young," says John Lydon, Sr. "He used to spend his holidays as my banksman. We were digging out cesspits and they were full of rats. When I would chuck out the dragline, the rats used to grab the rope and climb it back toward me. We had an agent there sometimes and he used to shoot them. But John would chuck them off with an ax."

The elder Lydon appears to be a robustly healthy man of fifty-four, his complexion ruddy and weathered by years of working the oil rigs in the North Sea. Margarite Byrne, Mr. Lydon's girlfriend and widow of his first cousin, divides her attention between the interview and the English version of *The Dating Game* on the living room telly. I tell him the story of John's piles.

"I didn't know this, you see," he says. "Even if it was true, he wouldn't tell me, because I would bring him back to school and sort it out. 'Cause if the master called him a liar in front of me, I'd smack him in the mouth."

You didn't actually smack the schoolmaster in the mouth, did you?

"But I would have. 'Cause I've been in pubs with John and I've had me jacket off more than once. All the time. I used to sort out all the problems in the pub. Whenever there was a row, I was the first one in it. Well, you know Irish people. They have a temper."

You would fight over John in the pubs?

"Regular it used to happen. In the pub across the street. We used to go there and you'd have girls come in and a girl would say, 'Hallo, Johnny, darling, can we have your autograph?' And then her boyfriend would call him a wanker. Then the punch-up started. I've had all me knuckles broken fighting there. John will tell you that himself. I've had three fights in one night."

Over John?

"Yeah, it's jealousy, isn't it? If anybody is famous at all, some girl wants to kiss him. Especially in the pub. That's where it all starts. When he comes home, we go to the pub. If there's a problem, we sort it out between us. We just have a go. Win or lose, what do you do? That's what life is all about, isn't it?"

Seems like it would make life difficult.

"No, not really. I'm hot-tempered, you see. I drive a heavy goods lorry in the city, and when you drive a truck down a narrow street, everybody is going like this to each other." Mr. Lydon makes what I always interpreted to be a "V" for victory sign but which means "up yours" in London. "And that's it, then. I have sort-outs in the streets every day. Every day I have a punch-up. Well, not every day. Most days I have a punch-up."

Mr. Lydon tells a long story about throttling another lorry driver who sneaked in front of him at a construction site and ended up bleeding in the gutter ("I don't see why I should let him slip me the mickey"). Sheba, the family dog, a muscular cross of Labrador and Doberman, grows restless and Margarite shoos her from the room.

"The dog has one fault," says Mr. Lydon. "If we take her out, she'll be walking along the green, calm as can be, and for no reason out of the blue she'll chomp on someone.

All of a sudden she's just got someone in her teeth, and she's got some teeth. Like a tiger. We just have her to keep the blacks away. Something about them that dogs don't like. I don't know what it is. Maybe it's the color of the skin."

The Lydons live in a two-story flat—the same in which Johnny grew up—in a housing estate (project) in the Finsbury Park section of London, a working-class Irish neighborhood that has in recent years become racially mixed. Of the four Lydon sons, two have been seriously hurt in fights, according to their father, with blacks.

"Jimmy was almost as famous as Johnny," says Mr. Lydon of his second eldest, standing proudly next to his pretty young wife and baby in a snapshot. "He had his own band, the 4″ Be 2″, you know. But he married a schoolteacher and she put the block on it. He's quite content now, painting and decorating."

One of Jimmy's first projects was his living room, which he redecorated like a pub in the green and gold colors of Ireland. Various aspects of his handiwork are displayed in the photographs, but it is hard to keep from looking at his face. His right eye socket is a grotesque mass of red scar tissue.

"He lost his eye about five years ago. He was at a stag party on a Friday night. He came out of the pub carrying a wedding present at half past three in the morning. When he got to the corner he met nine darkies. They said, 'What have you got in the bag?' He said, 'Aw, go away.' So they jumped him. Two of them picked up bottles and they both got him in the eye. Cut the eye clean out of his head. You've seen guys fight, but you've never seen anyone who could fight like Jimmy. Since he lost his eye, he's terrific. He's got the method, and he never loses, not now. If somebody cut your eye out, they'd never do it again to you, you'd make sure of that, wouldn't you?"

Bobby, the third eldest (the youngest, Martin, works for John as a roadie), has a semicircular, almost glowing red scar from just below his right earlobe to the corner of his mouth.

"It was August a year, a year last August. He was coming in at midnight and there was two colored guys playing their radio down there. And he sleeps in the front room, over the front door, and he said, 'Go away, it's a bit late to be shouting outside the door.' One went inside and the other said, 'What did you say, man?' Bobby said, 'You heard me. Piss off.' And as he turned around, the colored guy stuck a Stanley knife in his neck. Just nipped the jugular. When he come in, his head was hanging off him. You could see into his neck. We almost lost him, he lost so much blood. He's very lucky. Tough to control him afterward because he wanted to get the guys. He couldn't get the bloke who did it, because he's inside. Got three years. But Bobby got five of his mates. Caught them at the chip shop and gave them a good hiding."

Born in Galway, Ireland, Mr. Lydon moved to Scotland on his own at the age of fourteen, supporting himself on the pipelines and eventually working his way down to London. He met his wife there, the former Eileen Barry of Cork, at an Irish dance club.

"She was so quiet. It was funny: My son has a wife and she's exactly the same as mine is, Jimmy's wife is. And all she lives for is the baby and him. Nothing else in the world. And my wife was exactly the same. She idolized the children. Never wanted to go anywhere, just the children all the time. Except church. She was a really good Catholic. If there was a church that said mass twice a day, she'd make you go twice a day. She was a great Catholic. And as the lads grew up, they could never do anything wrong in her eyes. Anything. She backed Johnny all the way."

It was up to you to whack him when he got out of line?

"She'd never let you hit him. No way. You'd say, 'I'm going to give you a smack on the ear,' and she wouldn't let you touch him, no way. She'd say, 'Go away with your Irish temper and leave the lad alone.' They got on very well together, all the kids. But Johnny was more attached to her than anybody. It was always mum and John. She was so calm, she would sit down and talk to him for hours and hours. He wouldn't go nowhere without telling her. He wouldn't go outside the door without telling her where he was going. Maybe it was the meningitis that he got to depend on her so much.

"Johnny was eight years old when he had meningitis, you know. And he was in the hospital for months, I'd say three months. It's water on the brain, meningitis, isn't it? He kept getting pain in the back of his head. He used to have these lumbar punctures, you know, big needles into the spine, and they would draw the fluid. I used to have to hold him down on the bed when they gave him the lumbar punctures. He wouldn't let them give the lumbar punctures unless I was there. And he forgot everything in the hospital that he had learned in school. Lost his memory completely, couldn't remember who he was. And she taught him everything again herself. She was a genius at math, you know. You can have a calculator and she could do the problem in her head, and she could beat you to the answer. I'll be damned if I know where she learned it, but she could beat accountants with A-levels in mathematics."

When Johnny returned home, he lived mostly an indoors existence, reading books and listening to music alone in his room. There is a football (soccer) pitch right outside their back door, but even when he could be coaxed onto the field, he would refuse to kick the ball, just sort of waft his foot at it if it rolled directly to him. He was equally resistant to his formal education, getting expelled from Catholic school at the age of fourteen.

"It was a silly old master there, kept dictating to him," says Mr. Lydon. "Johnny had a bit of an accident, twisted his ankle one day. I took him up to casualty and they gave him a little card saying he'd been there. The master said he didn't want to hear any bloody excuses, didn't want to see it, it was all lies. They almost had a punch-up, you know what I mean, and he got expelled over it."

Johnny was standing there with a sprained ankle and a card from the hospital and the master wouldn't believe him?

"More or less called Johnny a lyin' b, and he got expelled."

Despite Mrs. Lydon prevailing on the Bishop of London to pay a surprise visit one Sunday morning ("I felt bad about it because you can't let the Bishop see you with a hangover, can you?") and promise to reinstate the lad, John transferred to Kingsbury College and fellow student Sid Vicious was soon a regular visitor to the Lydon home.

"My wife used to feed him here. She thought as much of Sid as she did of John, and Sid had never had nothing, really. I'd come home and if I'd had a few drinks, I'd say, 'Who's that wanker?' And she'd say, 'That's Johnny's friend. Leave off.' And she'd be pushing me out the door. I used to be a bit wild, you know. Martin, I'd pick him up and sling him under me arm. But she wouldn't let you do that. Even a colored person. If a colored person passed the door and he was hungry, she'd bring him in and give him a meal. She was that type. Me, I'd shoot him. The difference in people, it's unbelievable, isn't it?"

John and Sid went on to make history, causing hysteria on both sides of the Atlantic with the Sex Pistols, John getting thrown out of the band for being an asshole at the end of their brief American tour, Sid more or less murdering his girlfriend and committing suicide. The biggest blow to John, however, came in the fall of 1978, just after a trip to America with his mother to discuss plans for a solo career.

"She thought she had a tummyache from all the parties and food and drink. They couldn't find anything at the hospital, but she got bad and they opened her up and they discovered she had malignant cancer. He took it really bad. Because he was really attached to her, you know. He adored his mother. Really. From the meningitis. He set there all the time with her, day and night he set in the chair. The way he felt at the time was he thought it was all his problems that was causing this to her, his punk rock. But it wasn't. Cancer is a disease, and there's nothing you can do. We talked to four experts and they all said not even a miracle could cure her. He wouldn't believe the doctors couldn't do anything. I don't think he's trusted them since."

Wasn't he also mad at the priest?

"He was alcoholic. Before she died, she wanted to be anointed, and he was dead drunk at four o'clock in the afternoon. We'd been calling him all morning. Someone who goes to church every Sunday, and you can't get the priest to come when she's dying. She'd already been anointed four times because they expected her to die. They were giving her so many injections in trying to keep her alive that they were killing her. It seems like you could save people from suffering some of that agony and misery, but they won't let you."

Sheba the dog trots back into the living room looking for a little affection and Mr. Lydon gives her a pat on the head. "Only one bad habit our dog has," he says. "You mention the word *black* and she'll smash up against the window, trying to attack whoever's out there. She's prejudiced. She doesn't like colored people."

Johnny Rotten's solo career, it seems to me, can be characterized as a lot of trashing around looking for someone to blame for his pain. It has often been musically adventurous, but not very listenable unless you are into narcissism, despair, and scapegoating. Unlike his work with the Pistols, there is little funny about it. In his personal life, he has left many of his friends behind, angry and embittered and full of accusations that he lies. He seems more comfortable holding on to his enemies, like the Sex Pistols' manager Malcolm McLaren, always the mongoose to John's cobra, and recently John's victim in a court suit in which he and the surviving Pistols and Sid Vicious's mom won complete control of Glitterbest, McLaren's management company, and Matrixbest, McLaren's movie company. After a disastrous first album for Elektra in 1984 (a half-million-dollar advance and thirty thousand copies sold) and an equally disastrous tour, Rotten is again selling albums with *Album* and is going to assemble yet another version of his ever-shifting band, Public Image, Ltd., for a tour.

"I honestly didn't think this album would be commercial in any way," he says, sitting behind the desk of some absent executive at Virgin Records in London. "I thought it would be perceived as absolutely preposterous for me to delve into that kind of music, particularly using those guitars. I thought it would drive people against me, but it's done the exact opposite."

The first time I heard it, I thought you'd brought in Eddie Van Halen for the solos.

"He couldn't play that good. He'd have beaten it to death. Hah, hah, hah. I wanted to make a jolly good rock album, and that appeared to be the best way. I've worked with [producer] Bill Laswell before and we're a good team."

It's getting quite a bit of play in dance clubs, especially the single "Rise." When I heard the chorus—"May the road rise with you"—my first thought was, what's this guy doing in a good mood?

165

"Hah, hah, hah. I deserve to be. Hah, hah, hah. What a thing to say to me: 'You have no right to be happy. It's against all my preconceptions.' "

It is against all my preconceptions. Preconceptions based on getting verbally eviscerated, physically threatened, thoroughly embarrassed in previous meetings, recently hearing that you hit a friend of mine over the head with a beer can and shot blanks from a submachine gun at bystanders on the set of the video for "Rise" and—

"Got any cigarettes?" Rotten burps. "No? I'll go get some." Upon his return, I tell him I talked with his father. "What lies did he tell you? Did he get out the family snapshots?"

Some.

"My God. Was he currently in jail, or just getting out, or what?"

No. But all his stories were about giving someone a good hiding. He seemed proud of it.

"I know."

I got this vision of you as a small child in a house like that.

"Hah, hah, hah."

Obviously you know what I'm getting at.

"Yes. No comment. Hah, hah, hah. I definitely decided that was not going to be my life-style."

Another thing he talked about was the blacks who live in the estates.

"Oh, the race-hate nonsense. I can't stand that. Most of the working-class people here have that problem. It seems to be the only thing that unites them, their hatred for each other. It's outrageous. If it isn't against blacks, it's against people who live on the other side of the Thames, or Northerners and Southerners. It's just on and on and on. I am my own person. I wouldn't allow any of that nonsense to infiltrate my sensible brain, thank you."

A small child doesn't have a choice about that.

"It does, you know. I cannot be easily swayed. I've always felt what was right and what was wrong."

From the beginning you felt your father was wrong about black people? Or was there a single incident that turned your mind around?

"I don't think violence is the answer to anything," Rotten says but doesn't answer. "Never have, never will."

Two of your brothers were carved up by blacks.

"More coincidence than anything else. They're such raving loonies, the lot of them. They don't mind going out and scrapping with anybody or anything. I'd rather not talk about it. It depresses me, as it happens."

I found it kind of depressing, sitting there.

"I know—wondering when someone is going to turn on you."

I change the subject to his childhood meningitis.

"I blame it on the pork chops. I haven't eaten pork since. I was in a coma for a long time. I don't remember too much about it."

Your father held you down while you had your spinal shots?

"Yeah, that was bad. Every fucking six hours. That was torture. You can't imagine that thing."

Every six hours for how many days?

Every six hours for six months you got a hypodermic needle up your spine?

"Yeah. I nearly died."

Your father said that you'd forgotten everything you'd learned in school.

"That's true. I had to start all over again."

Your mother taught you your schooling?

"No, I taught myself. I'm self-taught."

At this point, Rotten whispers something to himself which I don't catch during the actual interview. Two weeks later, I play the tape back twelve times and Rotten is distinctly saying, "Don't you listen! I'm bored! Don't you listen!" For this I see three possible explanations: (1) He is possessed by Satan, who is not a fan of psychoanalysis; (2) he is commanding himself not to listen because questions about his mom are painful; and (3) he thinks I don't listen and finds the entire interview a snore. In any case, his manager, perhaps by extrasensory perception, seems to pick up on Explanation #3 and interrupts with a suggestion that we finish, which I do by asking if he's seen his family lately.

"They're doing all right. They're still fighting."

It's a hell of a way to get through life.

"You can't change them. They won't have it. They're self-righteous about it."

What I'm trying to figure out is why you're different.

"I can fight if I'm pushed into it. I've had very good training."

Yeah, but your face is not a mass of scar tissue.

"And it won't be."

SIDEBAR

"Energy has been missing from music for so long," notes John Lydon, "particularly in England, where it's all nail varnish and Nancy-boy keyboards, which people have been trying to break away from for some time." Clearly, the PiL leader sees *Album* as just such a breakaway, one which he feels returns to "my own little mine" of the Sex Pistols and first Public Image releases in terms of pure rock energy.

Having established a "brilliant" working relationship with Bill Laswell on "World Destruction," the

Afrika Bambaataa/Lydon twelve-inch, Lydon again tabbed Laswell to coproduce *Album* under a shared "umbrella theory." Explains Lydon, whose goal was an "up-tempo, nondisco"-sounding record, "We both like to cover a lot of musical ground," and Laswell indeed brought his customary far-reaching worldview to the project.

Noting that the recording was "well thought out in advance" and "definitely organized but with room to improvise," Laswell says that the finished product was a team effort guided by specific musical "reference points." For the record, the musicians enlisted were Ryuichi Sakamoto, keyboards; Bernie Worrell, organ; Nicky Skopelitis, six- and twelve-string guitars; Steve Vai, guitar; Malachi Favors, acoustic bass; Bernard Fowler, background vocals; L. Shankar, violin; Ginger Baker, drums; Tony Williams, drums; Aiyb Dieng, percussion; Jonas Hellborg, electric bass; and Steve Turre, didjeridoo. As for the reference points, Laswell names Led Zeppelin for its "sound and attitude," as well as Zulu music, Joujouka, and other North and South American musics, while Lydon singles out the Stooges' *Fun House*.

"There was a definite plan to make a more rock-oriented record, more direct and musical than past PiL records," continues Laswell. "But even though we were dealing with a simple beat and chord changes, we didn't want to use just rock clichés. And while there was a basic direction, the musicians were given a lot of freedom. I think that the total sound shows the personality of the individual musicians."

The recording process itself, says Lydon, was "very quick," taking three weeks of one-take recording time "in every studio in New York" and one week of mixing. "We were determined to get the best drum sound we could, but that doesn't come cheaply. We had an awful budget. Ridiculous. Arcadia gets eight hundred thousand, and we had two-sixteenths of that. Outrageous!"

According to Laswell, the drums were recorded at the Power Station by Jason Corsaro, who also mixed the entire album there. "It was necessary to record the drums with a particular engineer with a big drum sound," explains Laswell, who adds that Vai's guitar was recorded at Electric Ladyland because of its "historical resonance and good larger room sound on a live amp." Additional recording was done at RPM Sound Studios and Quadrasonic Sound Systems, Robert Musso engineering all but the drum tracks.

"It was like the good old days," says Lydon of the swift recording pace. "We went for high energy and instant reaction. I could play the master before editing and it sounded perfectly finished."

Laswell now looks ahead to forming a musical "continuum" using the same musicians and stylistic relationships established in *Album*. "It's the beginning of something that you'll hear in future projects," he says, noting a commitment by the PiL collaborators to work together again and solidify their initial undertaking. Reporting that his most recent production of a forthcoming Motorhead album continues in his current harder rock direction, Laswell says that there may even be a Ginger Baker solo album using many of the PiL players.

— Jim Bessman

June 1986

GUNS N' ROSES

ARE OUTLAWS, AND

EVERYONE HAS

GUNS N' ROSES

BY MARK ROWLAND

If I'd gone on through school," Axl Rose says, "I'd probably be a lawyer. Then I could take half the people who screw with me to court. I was watching this show the other day with four top criminal lawyers, and they talked about feeling how, when they're in a courtroom, it's like them against the world. I feel that way too: There's always a million obstacles up to the time you go onstage, times I don't even want to go on. Once I'm there I don't know where it comes from, but it's like, 'Boy, this is great.'

Even if you're having a terrible time, you're just jazzed that you made it."

Texas Stadium, Dallas, and not a ten-gallon in sight. Back in the concrete bowels of the arena, where leathered rockers and their roadies confab with potbellied security guards and limo drivers, the sound from the stage is a blotch of noise. Out on the field it's about the same, only louder.

It's a hot afternoon with a tease of rain, like a barbecue pit that occasionally sizzles. Forty thousand kids are having a wingding, sampling an international pop smorgasbord that includes Ziggy Marley, Iggy Pop, and headliners INXS.

Running second on the bill is Hollywood garage band Guns N' Roses, whose first album, *Appetite for Destruction*, has unexpectedly sold over six million copies, and whose "Sweet Child o' Mine" is currently the nation's top-selling single. It's their last gig in a nine-month tour, a chance to go out in a blaze of glory. There's just one problem: They don't want to be here. They're tired, they're cranky, they hate INXS. As usual, they're not shy about venting their feelings. "What can they do," says guitarist Izzy Stradlin, "kick us off the tour?"

An afterthought of Hurricane Gilbert starts to drizzle over the thousands as Guns N' Roses—Axl, Izzy, lead guitarist Slash, bassist Duff McKagan, and drummer Steve Adler—crank into "It's So Easy," their paean to the wild life; it's all they can do to move around without falling on the slippery stage. They can't hear through their monitors, but keep slogging through "Mr. Brownstone" (Izzy's "little ditty about heroin"), a ballad called "Patience" ("Guess I could use a little, huh?" says Axl by way of introduction), a bluesy instrumental rave-up from Slash and the band's anthem, "Welcome to the Jungle."

It's a mess, but it works. Back in the bleachers, the

faithful are singing along to every indecipherable word as girls in various articles of Guns N' Roses–wear scream just like in old Beatles movies while their guys pump their fists. Onstage, the band's still pissed. "Guess nobody wants to play today," booms Axl before taking soccer practice with one of the monitors. Next up is "Sweet Child," the crowd screaming, "Where do we go?" with gospel fervor, as if Axl knew the answer. Then it's "Paradise City," and as quickly as they came the band is out of here, Duff smashing his bass in frustration, Slash cursing because he doesn't have a guitar to smash—"They forgot to bring a cheap one." We're less than forty minutes into a scheduled seventy-five-minute set. "Does it get any worse than this?" someone asks backstage, missing the point. At their worst, Guns N' Roses are real, and it connects. Back on the field the crowd's still cheering.

An hour later the band relaxes in the high-roller boxes along the loge, knocking back a few beers and shrugging off the damage while INXS clamors below. Axl, however, is still agitated.

"If Michael Hutchence says anything about me, I'll go back down there and kick his ass!" Axl becomes more meditative. "I hope we learned a major lesson from this: Don't do something for money 'cause it ain't gonna work. We agreed to do this show a long time ago, and we've been dreading it ever since. When we finally got out onstage, it just hit us like a ton of bricks: Who the hell are we foolin'?"

"Usually when we get in that situation, we get very punk," says Slash. "We blaze, even if we don't play that good, 'cause we get so energetic. But we didn't do that today. We cracked. We didn't take over. The promoters, the bookers, they want us to keep going. We've been getting offers to headline the Forum, Madison Square Garden. But we knew this had to end. And Axl's voice is getting to the point where he can't keep going." Slash flashes a smile. "Everybody's been having a good time; the thing is, we're burned out."

In a little more than the year since the release of *Appetite for Destruction*, Guns N' Roses has become the most popular band in America. Fighting their way out of the remnants of L.A.'s Spandex scene, they've been heralded as, variously, avatars of Eighties rock, pop, heavy metal, and even punk, inasmuch as punk was always more an attitude than a musical style. Slagged by the PMRC and by Keith Richards (neither of whom were even addressing their music), they have a way of attracting controversy. Their life-styles are reflected in their songs—not necessarily celebrated, but presented without apology.

"Sex and drugs and rock 'n' roll" was a Fifties taboo, a Sixties credo, a Seventies cliché; in the climate of Reaganbush, AIDS, and MTV, it's a taboo all over again. That's what really fuels Guns N' Roses' celebrity, critics carp. The record company says it's just selling records, the boys in the band say they're just being themselves, and the little girls understand.

Lost in the shuffle are five individuals who write songs, play instruments, rehearse, tour, scuffled for years, and must now grapple with the expectations stardom brings. You can't separate their lives from their music (in many ways their lives define their music), but above all, Guns N' Roses is a band, and for all their personal screwups, its members have made the most of it. Hanging together so well, one suspects, is about all that's kept some of them from hanging very separately.

Slash (Saul Hudson) walks into the neighborhood Hamburger Hamlet and orders a double Stoli with o.j. "I've been up since five this morning doing phone interviews," he says. "Guy called me from Brazil. The album's fourteen months old and it just opened at Number Seven in Brazil and Greece, and in Holland it's like Number Ten. So I've had to do all this. . . ."

Slash is deceptively dissolute. He's not only the band's best musician and a talented artist—he designed Guns N' Roses' logo—he's also helped chart the group's course from the start. "I'm a real workaholic when it comes to that. Anything else, I'm lazy. I worked my ass off to promote the band in the beginning, get us from spot to spot on the club scene. Making fliers and phone calls and screw the right people. . . . I'm pretty levelheaded and don't make too many dumb decisions. We negotiated our own record deal. We're very conscientious about what we do and how we do it." When it comes to constructing their music, Slash says his attitude is "aggressive. I come up with the majority of the riffs, Axl the majority of melodies and lyrics, and Izzy will come up with really good chords. We work together, so everybody enjoys doing it. But I'm very adamant if I hear a riff in my head; I hear the whole band and then I want to reproduce that."

Slash grew up in England; his father designed album covers for Geffen Records, his mother clothes for artists like David Bowie and the Pointer Sisters. Surrounded by pop music, he liked everything from the Jefferson Airplane to Minnie Riperton, but the Stones, Zeppelin, Beck, Faces, and Aerosmith were "major. When I was fourteen I was over at this girl's house who I'd been trying to pick up for months and she played *Aerosmith Rocks*. I listened to it eight times and forgot all about her." He credits Jimmy Page as his biggest influence—"that bluesy sound. And I've always been a real riffs person.

"Before Izzy, I'd never been able to play with another guitarist. Axl was the only guy on the whole L.A. scene who could sing, and there was no getting Izzy away from Axl. The funny thing about Izzy and I is that we each play what

177

we want, and sometimes it works and sometimes it doesn't. It can be frustrating for me because he's very stubborn. He plays a very lightweight, sort of Keith Richards style, whereas if I want a heavy riff, I'll want us both to play it to make it really stick out. There's a lot of songs on our album I'm really not happy with that way. 'Welcome to the Jungle,' for instance. Sometimes Duff will beef it up, like the riff in 'Paradise City.' I'm a little more knowledgeable on guitar; Izzy's a good songwriter with a great sense of style.

"Guns N' Roses is sort of like, we were the only five people in L.A. that could enjoy what each other did enough to start a band and keep it together. Part of the magic is that we're like this mirror of what kids really go through, what the reality of being a teenager is about, having to work nine-to-five and having shitty parents and dealing with cops, authority. So we're very close to the kids we play for. That's what rock 'n' roll is for me, a kind of rebellious thing, getting away from authority figures, getting laid maybe, getting drunk, doing drugs at some point. We're that kind of band and there's not too many others. There's tons of rock concerts that are about as safe as pie! For a rock show we are doing something more unpredictable, that has a certain amount of . . . recklessness. We're very fresh with it."

Slash grins and orders another vodka double, his fourth. His father, he mentions in passing, was an alcoholic. "This sounds sort of childish," he says, "but I have to drink a certain amount before we go onstage or I'm awkward and I can't play right. Otherwise I'm too jittery. But a lot of people see me hanging around clubs drunk off my ass, and they think that's all we're about. We get this image for being irresponsible punks who don't care about anything. Well, we are sort of like that, but we don't do it on purpose, we're just being young! I think the Stones were like that."

Well, one of the Stones died. And you have a reputation for careening pretty close to the edge yourself.

"Our drug situation's not as bad as it was," says Slash, a little more reservedly. "Yeah, I have been out a few times—'blue' and all that. We used to sing 'Knockin' on Heaven's Door'; that's dedicated to my best friend Todd, who died in a hotel room a while back. We'd copped some stuff and he got it right there. I tried to bring him back . . . and he was like my best, best friend.

"That really scared me. I had a habit and I finally stopped it. And every so often, I'll chip, you know, just for the fun of it. But that's not something you talk about because you don't want people to think, 'He's a drug addict.'

"I'm not promiscuous like I used to be, either. 'Cause I worry about AIDS, and also you burn out on it. It's not that big a thing. And so now, what do I do?" He smiles engagingly. "We're at the MTV awards and I meet Traci Lords—and we went out the other night." He shakes his head in disbelief. "I'm a parody of my own life-style, I'll tell ya."

The other week he leased his first apartment; before that he'd been living out of a hotel. He rents the apartment adjacent to his friend Ronnie's, a crew member who doubles as his chauffeur and bodyguard. Slash spends a lot of time in his room. "I have quiet. Well, I still don't have quiet; I mean, guys from Brazil are calling me at five in the morning. But it's work-oriented, so I'm happy. I sit in bed with the TV turned down, staring at the ceiling, coming up with stuff in my head, trying to make things work. I put a lot of ideas on tape. It never stops with me, twenty-five hours a day, Guns N' Roses. And I can sit there and practice and get all my material I've put together over the last nine months and start setting goals for our next record. Getting drunk and going out with Traci Lords and stuff is just what

I do in my time off. I'm a very day-to-day person. 'Cause that's how we've been living for a while."

The studio is ready. The photographer has set up the lights; the assistants have stocked the freezer with Stoli and beer. Now there's little to do but wait for Axl. And wait. The photographer has flown back from Cape Canaveral just for this, unaware that getting the five members of Guns N' Roses together for anything but a gig or a party means bucking heavy odds. An hour passes; two hours. So far only Izzy has arrived; Duff, Steve, and Slash call in periodically to see if anyone's heard from Axl. Dream on.

"The first thing I remember about Axl," Izzy is saying— "this is before I knew him—is the first day of class, eighth or ninth grade, I'm sitting in class and I hear this noise going on in front, and I see these fucking books flying past, and I hear this yelling, and there's this scuffle and then I see him, Axl, and this teacher bouncing off a doorjamb. And then he was gone, down the hall, with a whole bunch of teachers running after him. That's the first thing," Izzy laughs. "I'll never forget it."

Stradlin has the gaunt, classic look of a guy who was born to play guitar. When he's in the mood he radiates a kind of shy charm, and he punctuates his stories with droll, cynical humor. "When I was eleven or twelve I had this friend whose older brothers were like hooligans; they rode bikes, would get drunk and fight all the time, and they'd have these bands play at this big farmhouse, it was like an airplane hangar. So I'd be hanging out there, getting shitfaced, and after a while they'd be so drunk they couldn't even play and they'd go, 'C'mon up here, little kid, and play the drums!' So that was the first adrenaline rush. Other than that my life was completely boring."

Izzy grew up in Indiana, "so far out in Bumfuck I could drive to somebody's house for ten miles all on dirt roads." His parents split up when he was a teenager; he moved with his mother to the larger burg of Lafayette, where he and Axl eventually met and formed their first garage band. They were into punk, and Lafayette's bars only had room for country and cover bands, "which we hated at the time. When you're sixteen and you live out there you hate everything you see."

After trying his luck in Chicago and Indianapolis, Izzy threw his drums into the back of a Chevy Impala and headed for L.A. Within three days he was in a band—"since I had a car and a drum kit, I was an asset"—whose next gig was in a downtown warehouse. "We're getting ready to go on," Stradlin recalls, "and these guys show up completely in drag! I mean, lipstick, eye liner, pink Spandex, Afros . . . this was my band! They didn't tell me there was a motif, you know? And it was like, slam music, one-two-three-four. We made it through about three songs, and then all these skinheads were onstage spitting and beating the fuck out of the band. I took a cymbal stand, took a few swings, and was out the back door.

"That kind of broke me into the way things were out here. After that I had no problems with how anyone looked or sounded, or if they didn't like you. So I guess it was a good way to break the ice."

That was 1979. The next year, Easter morning, "Axl shows up on my front door, soaking wet with a backpack. He'd been looking for me for about a month. He didn't know how big this place was." A couple of years later, Izzy was playing guitar and they were living in Hollywood, "slumming it here and there. We started writing songs in this roach-infested pad off Franklin Avenue. We were doing speed like there was no tomorrow, and night after night we would just pump out this fast, upbeat, insane music. Slapped together a band, and I'd tell club owners we were playing parties and could easily bring in five hundred people. When twenty would show up they'd get really upset and we'd never get paid. But we were slowly getting it together."

The band, Hollywood Rose, eventually broke up. When Izzy and Axl reunited, they decided, "Let's not waste any more time. We moved up in life, to West Hollywood," Izzy jokes, "and met Slash and Steve and Duff. It's funny, before I even met Slash I'd seen this drawing he made of Aerosmith in a music store. And I thought, 'I gotta meet this guy.'

"Once we got that lineup together, everything we did revolved around the music. I think 'cause we were all so fed up, that was all we thought about. It's still that way— so if we disappear tomorrow, at least the music's there."

Stradlin is the closest thing in the band to a loner; when he's on tour he likes to wander the streets by himself, and his girlfriend mentions he'd like to buy a house in the desert. But with success, he says, "I enjoy life more now, I'm not so pissed off all the time. When you got no bread, drug problems, no money, and winos in your alley throwing up, it does tend to aggravate you. It's much better now. I can live like a normal person. I mean, for the ten years I lived here, I never had a bed. I just bought one, and it's a futon. I guess I'm used to lying on the floor."

One night during their recent tour, Izzy saw his father for the first time in eight years. "He comes walking backstage unannounced, completely out of the blue. Took a second or two to recognize him. It was a real trip. But it was definitely not"—he catches the thought, brings it back home—"well, I don't want to get into it.

"I mean, in ten years I've only been back to Indiana twice. I don't even know anyone there anymore, I don't keep in touch like Axl does. But when I look back, I do see some kind of stability that comes from growing up in a fucking cornfield. You're at one with the earth," Izzy laughs. "You don't give a shit about much. It's a simple life."

How does that explain Axl? "Well, that has a lot to do with how he was brought up and how he sees things. He's very uncompromised. He's the first one to say, 'Fuck this.' "

As if to prove the point, Axl never shows up for the photo shoot. After three hours Izzy decides he'd better hit the road. "I know this guy," he says. "If I don't leave now and he does show up, we'll have to wait five hours next time."

Vicki Hamilton is an A&R woman at Geffen Records. Her beat is the street, more specifically, the sprawling L.A. club scene where she's discovered acts like Motley Crue and Poison. She wasn't yet at Geffen when she spotted Guns N' Roses playing at the Troubadour for about a hundred fans; watching the show, Vicki found herself with "the feeling I get in my stomach when I see a band that's going to make it. I watched them for three months and I remember thinking, 'Why isn't anybody [in the industry] going for this?' After meeting the band, I knew. They were definitely outlaws. And I thought, 'This may kill me, but they're so great, I have to do it.' "

The band, she recalls, was living in a one-room apartment that doubled as a rehearsal space; they'd built bunk beds above the floor. "There was a girl over there one night, and she wouldn't leave Axl alone, and he got pissed, so he ripped off her clothes, threw her out, and locked the door. So she went to the cops and said he raped her." The upshot was that Axl ended up living in Hamilton's apartment—*The Fugitive*—and when the police raided their studio, the rest of the band followed. They stayed four months while the band negotiated its record deal. "I had four or five labels throwing bids," says Hamilton, "and the dollars were getting bigger."

Tom Zutaut, Geffen's head of A&R, signed Guns N' Roses to a $75,000 advance. Hamilton, who was trying to sign a contract to manage, was cut loose by the band, and eventually sued to get back $10,000 she'd invested in them. She did get a job with Geffen, though, and says she's managed to retain good relations with the band—save one member.

"Axl won't talk to me. Why? Maybe because I sued them, but I gave up trying to figure him out years ago. There are times when he's the sweetest boy you could know, but when he gets mad, he's like a top spinning off. He's not consistently evil," she laughs sharply. "And he's not consistently nice, either. It's two distinct personalities, that's what's so scary.

"But you're talking about street creatures. They had never had any money before and suddenly it was like, 'Life's a party now.' The day they signed I was crying because I knew what was lying ahead."

Such was the crucible in which Guns N' Roses created their aptly titled *Appetite for Destruction.* "A very heavy drug period for the band," Izzy says frankly. "A lot of the music is a reflection of that. There's always a lot of abuse going on in Hollywood, but at that time it was like we were in the middle of a pinwheel."

As rock 'n' roll stories go, this part's not unique. But what makes *Appetite for Destruction* special isn't simply the band's penchant for extreme experience but its ability to reflect it in the songs without wallowing in romanticism or cheap sentiment. The power of a song like "Mr. Brownstone," which Izzy admits he wrote "in about five minutes, while I was cooking something up," is in the way it evokes not only the thrill of the fast lane (the Bo Diddleyish rhythm) but also, through Axl's frantic cadences, its implicit terror. No matter how far-flung the band's other themes—the come-hither decadence of "Welcome to the Jungle," the prayer for deliverance in "Paradise City," the paranoia of "Out to Get Me," or the wary hopes expressed in "Sweet Child o' Mine"—the point of view is invariably existential. The songs supply no answers but ask plenty of questions.

Axl's remarkable vocal shifts from song to song really do suggest multiple personae, projected with near-palpable intensity. Slash's guitar solos are emblems of flash and taste, skimming acrobatically off Izzy's angular, quirky chord changes. All would make their mark in any event—but check out the melodic, understated bass lines of Duff McKagan, whose steady propulsion plays off Steve Adler's happy-go-lucky drum patterns while anchoring the overall sound.

"None of us are the greatest musicians, you know," says McKagan. "We all have big technical holes. But what puts us apart from other bands is that it's always rough and real. We'll never be like Rush; we'll never be that good! But I think we're way more honest. In some ways it's a calling of a rebel spirit to kids. 'Cause we always do what we want."

With the album's release Guns N' Roses hit the highway, opening for Iron Maiden, Motley Crue, and finally Aerosmith, which comes as close as any band to being Guns N' Roses' role model. "We hate to admit it," Slash admits, "but they are sort of like teenage heroes." In concert together, Aerosmith were more polished by far, but Guns N' Roses thrashed out the drama of its members' lives, and Axl's Janis Joplin–like stage presence connected on a deeper emotional level. By tour's end they were openers in name only, drawing half the crowds and running away with the T-shirt concessions. Record sales: no contest.

As the group's popularity ballooned, so did its bad-boy reputation, to the point where some members began to feel like cartoon characters. "It worries me," Izzy says, "when these kids would come up and try to give me coke and

185

stuff. I'd go, 'Uh, no, thanks, not this part of the tour.' 'Cause the first two months you go for it, and the next thing you know they're dragging you onstage from the bus."

"You know, I really liked it when the kids loved us and we were still sort of underground," says Slash. "Now it's gotten to the point where we're sort of a circus act for normal society to go, 'Look at them fall down. Isn't that cute?' Sometimes it just pisses me off. I always thought of us as basically nice guys who were overexaggerated about. I mean, we don't rob banks, we don't beat up girls, we don't smash guitars over kids' heads in the front rows. I don't see why it's such a crime to be us.

"The fact is, we're all really sensitive people. And that's probably why, for one, I drink so much, why Axl flies off the handle and has these huge fits of total depression. Because we're still living life, and sometimes that's hard to deal with.

"There's no big macho sense in this band. Duff's married; Axl's got a girlfriend he loves very much. Maybe sometimes we have relationships or other things that just drive us crazy. No one wants to know about that, though. Because at this point, it's not 'Guns N' Roses' for any of that to happen."

Days go by; no Axl. Notes are dropped at the hotel where he's living with girlfriend Erin Everly, the inspiration for "Sweet Child." He's spotted around town, hanging out with Slash at a party, cutting background vocals for Don Henley, helping to put the final mixes on the acoustic tracks for Guns N' Roses' forthcoming EP. He dodges a second photo shoot, ducks an interview appointment. Nothing personal, it's explained, it's just Axl's way.

Vicki Hamilton recalls that on the day Guns N' Roses were slated to begin their tour with Aerosmith, no one knew where Axl was or even if he'd make the gig. People were sitting in the Hard Rock Café taking bets on it. He finally appeared, an hour before showtime. Much later, toward the end of that tour, Axl approached Guns N' Roses' gregarious road manager Doug Goldstein, concerned, Goldstein says, that others felt he'd become a prima donna. "I haven't changed, have I, Doug?" "Of course not," Goldstein replied affectionately. "You've always been a prick."

That's pretty much the attitude regarding Axl, frustration mitigated by sympathy and respect. Maybe because he's so valued as a gifted (and lucrative) artist, maybe because all the tales of drugs and debauchery surrounding the band have disguised more serious problems related to Axl's mercurial temperament. Sources around him say he's on drugs—the prescriptive variety—to alleviate symptoms of manic depression. Sometimes he doesn't take them. And one thing everyone agrees on: No one tells Axl what to do. The result is that one can never be sure where Axl Rose will show up, and, if he does, which Axl will show.

And one afternoon, Axl does appear—a thoughtful and amiable Axl, with some time on his hands before popping over to a party for George Michael, of all people. "I've read reviews where people who like us say we're not the kind of band that'll be caught spinning *Faith*. And I used to have that attitude, before I started listening to the record over and over. Now all I know is that, listening to his record, it'll teach you how to deal with women."

The subject of women brings to mind the first *Appetite for Destruction* album cover, pulled by Geffen (and now, of course, a collector's item) after protests that its imagery condoned sexual violence toward women.

"We didn't put that out to outrage people," Axl protests. "I thought it was a very cool piece of art that would stand the test of time. I don't think it was encouraging sexual abuse at all. I think it's an idea in people's heads that she

187

is attractive, a sexual fantasy. Like, this poor girl got abused and you're thinking about how your husband wants to fuck her, so you're upset. People get scared of their own thoughts."

What thoughts scare you?

"That people are always trying to provoke some kind of fight so they can sue me. I'm scared of thrashing an asshole and going to jail for it. For some reason I can walk into a room and someone will pick a fight. That's always happening with me.

"Like, I went into a store once to buy a stun gun. We were headlining the Whiskey and things were getting out of hand, so I figured, 'I'll buy stun guns. We won't have to break their jaw; we'll just zap 'em and carry them out.' So my brother and I walked into the store and I said, 'Excuse me, sir, can I see this stun gun, please?' Being polite. And the guy goes, 'Listen, son. I don't need your bullshit!' And my brother says, 'Listen, he just got signed, he can buy ten of these,' and the guy says, 'I don't care, I'll sell them to you but not to him.'

"That happens to me a lot. If I'm breaking the law, fine. But when I'm just being a nice guy . . ."

Axl's delicate features and slender physique bely his notoriety as a hellion. Back in Indiana, he says, he was thrown in jail at least twenty times, though he never did anything worse than get drunk and rowdy. "I was one of the craziest of my friends, but also one of the smartest, so they figured I was the ringleader. They never got me for anything, though. Once this girl picked me up in a car; she was sixteen or seventeen and her mom reported it stolen. The police tried to get me for grand theft auto, contributing to the delinquency of a minor, statutory rape—and I didn't touch the girl! After they filed the charges I went over to her house and we had a party. Then I left town."

He started singing in church at age five, the oldest child

of three in a family of Holy Rollers. "It was in the country; you'd get up and sing old gospel songs and hymns and gospel hits of the Seventies. I loved to work on harmonies. I was always getting in trouble in choir practice for singing everybody else's parts."

Axl won Bible contests, taught Sunday school, played the piano. He saw amazing religious occurrences, miracles, but became disappointed when nothing happened to him. Secular music became the true revelation. He acquired eclectic pop tastes; to develop his singing, he locked himself in the bathroom every day and sang along with Nazareth albums and *The Eagles' Greatest Hits*. Now he likes to listen to Ennio Morricone and old Sinatra records.

Writing songs, "I try not to follow any rules. Slash'll sit with his guitar and I'll run through ideas as he plays; we connect the pieces together. We push each other. Izzy and I write real quick off the top of our heads. We write a lot of fun stuff." Lyrics, though, require solitude. "I want to write about some of the situations I've seen and types of people I've met in the last two years, and I don't want anyone to influence that. People look over your shoulder and say, 'I don't know if you should say that, man, that's a little heavy,' but I don't want to be censored before I bring the song to the band."

There are songs on an upcoming EP, he says, that will probably "freak people out." Axl's decided to deal with it by writing a note of explanation/apology on the album cover. He also mentions that he recently bought a custom Corvette. "It's got a Chevy engine, a four-cam that goes a hundred and eighty-plus miles an hour. I'll join a racetrack where they'll teach you how to drive it fast. I like the idea of having a car where I won't be so eager to put my gun in the car and shoot somebody."

Oh. And how are you dealing with success?

"Right now it's hard. It's gonna take a little time from

living like a rat in the streets to being able to manage my accounts, find places to live, buy houses. I'm getting a place here and in the Midwest, and eventually I'd like to live in New York, and get ideas for songs on the street. But right now I'm just trying to move real fast, get this crap out of the way, and get myself stable, 'cause we have another record to make, and I really want to make that record. It's like a dream: We get to be 'the big talented artists,' respected by people in the business. I hope to do as much material as possible, maybe a double album. So if anything happens to the band, it'll still live on for a while. Right now I think it's too early for people on the outside to really tell what we're all about.

"I hope I'll be really satisfied after that. I don't want to go solo, but there are areas I'd like to explore—maybe movies—where I might not be able to stay in the band to do it. So I'm not going to say we'll be around forever, but I hope I'll write the kind of music that sticks around for a long time, whether you hear it on the radio or not. That's what I want, to be part of a band that gets a little place in history."

The way he says it gives the thought weight; Axl is the kind of guy who seems almost uncomfortably alert to changes in the weather, to the sensitivity of a lyric, the nuance of a song, a sudden shift of mood. . . . "Only because I react to everything," he says quietly. "I react to thoughts. I can be sitting here in a good mood and think about something really fucked, and I can't get it out of my head, I'll react to it. If I hold it back, I walk around frustrated for a very long period of time. When I talk with an interviewer, it hurts my feelings if they act like my best friend, then chop me down. I always try to let people know what they want when we're talking.

"I think I'm growing. I have more insights into things.

I know when I listen to music, I really want something to be there. Like, I hated Metallica, but then everyone started talking about them, so I bought their records. And the song that really caught me was 'Fade to Black.' I got addicted to that song. It was the only thing I could put on at the end of the day, which was usually around dawn. It's a song about suicide, but I would put it on before I went to sleep and it would make me relax. For some reason it made me want to try harder. I'd think, 'Yeah, I can get up and face tomorrow.'

"The only thing that worries me about death is, I have this record to make and I'll be really pissed off if I die before I make it. After that I won't give a shit. That's when it's gonna get dangerous."

AMPS N' AXES

Guitarist **Slash** says he's still "paying off a guy a hundred dollars a week" for a '59 Gibson Les Paul he played on *Appetite for Destruction* and in concert; he has several other guitars, like the '59, all Les Pauls and equipped with Seymour Duncan pickups, including two '68 black beauties and a '56 gold top. He cranks them through Marshall amps. And that's it.

Izzy Stradlin also plays Gibsons, but through Mesa/Boogie amps. "I get this growling kind of sound, a little twangy." He's also lately been playing custom guitars and pickups made by Bill Lawrence.

Duff McKagan usually plays the same bass live that he uses on the record, an '85 Fender Jazz special; he also has a similar model by Kramer. He uses two Gallien-Krueger 800RP heads, one two-by-fifteen cabinet with Peavey four-hundred-watt speakers and a two-by-fifteen Gallien-Krueger cabinet with Peavey two-hundred-watt speakers.

Steve Adler plays Tama drums and Sabian cymbals. No special microphones for **Axl Rose**, says road manager Doug Goldsmith: "He breaks too many."

December 1988

THE ALLMAN

BROTHERS IN

"THE FOOT-SHOOTIN'

PARTY" (A TALE OF

THE OLD SOUTH)

BY BILL FLANAGAN

■

When I was a young man,

my friend Paco took a job road-managing the Allman

Brothers Band. Although southern rock was not my

cup of gumbo, my friend's enthusiasm lured me into

the Allmans' company on several occasions. The first

time I was introduced to Gregg Allman, a man of con-

siderable charm and inconsistent attention span, he

said, "Mister Flanagan, I'm glad to finally meet you!

I've heard you're one of the few people in this business

who knows what's real and what's bullshit and how

to tell the difference!" Gee, I thought, I'll have to give "Whippin' Post" another shot. Gregg and I spent the whole night hanging out, going to a jam session, a party, and finally back to his hotel, where he played songs on an acoustic guitar until dawn. The next time I saw Gregg, he greeted me by saying, "Mister Flanagan, I'm glad to finally meet you!"

One cold winter night after an Allmans concert at Boston Garden, I found myself in the back of a long black limousine with Gregg and the group's guitarist, Dickey Betts. I don't think the two of them were getting along very well. Those who knew more than me about the Allmans claimed there was a sort of sibling rivalry between Gregg, younger brother of the band's late leader Duane Allman, and Betts, who'd been Duane's protégé. Maybe that was true. Or maybe (for this was late in the band's first incarnation) they were just sick of each other. Gregg talked constantly as we rode along. Betts just stared out the window.

Gregg was complaining about the war in Vietnam. "That was a war that we had nothing to do with," he declared. "Many lives taken, many families broken, for absolutely no reason at all. I shot a bullet through my foot so I wouldn't have to go. A .22 Saturday Night Special. We had a foot-shootin' party, me and my brother."

"You and Duane shot yourselves?" I asked.

"No," Gregg said. "He got called first. I took him to the induction center and he had on a pair of pink panties. He was swishin' and sayin' "—Gregg affected a lisping voice— " 'Where's my pistol? I want to shoot those bastards!'

"He came out to the car at halftime crying. My brother didn't cry very much but they had him scared to death, man. There's the goddamn bus waitin' there to take his ass away after he raises his hand. He said, 'Man, it didn't work.' "

Dickey Betts turned his head slowly toward Gregg with a look of amazement.

"Who are you talkin' about, Gregg?" Betts asked.

"Duane."

Betts eyes narrowed. "You sayin' Duane wore pink panties?"

"To the *induction center.*"

"Oh!" Betts, obviously relieved, turned his attention back to the window.

Greg returned to his story: "The army didn't buy this pink panties shit at all. Duane came to the car and he was weepin'. I said, 'Ah, shit, man. *Just tell 'em you ain't gonna fuckin' go! That's it!'*

"He said, 'Yeah, that's really gonna work, you dumb shit!' But sure enough, he went in there and, come down to the end of it where you raise your right hand to take the oath, Duane put his hand in his pocket. The sergeant was screamin' in his ear, 'You son of a bitch! I'll see your ass in Leavenworth!' Duane said, 'No! No, I'm not goin' over there to kill people I don't even know don't even know why I'm doin' it! No!'

"They said, 'All right, you go on home. We'll see you in court. You'll be bustin' rocks at Leavenworth. We'll get you ten to twenty.'

"Well, they lost his file. He never heard from 'em. But he was sweatin' there for a few months.

"Then I got my 'Greetings.' We had just had our first chance to record. Duane said, 'Shit, man! What do you mean gettin' drafted?' That's the way he was. I said, '*I* didn't send the letter! Don't get on my case! You were lucky! They lost your file! I might not be so damn lucky! Now tell me what I'm gonna do. This is serious. There's a damn *war* goin' on!' This is when they were pickin' names on TV. My birthday was the first damn one they picked. Bingo. First damn Ping-Pong ball. I was watchin' it on TV and I said, 'Shit.' By this time I'd heard about napalm and all.

"I spent the first afternoon gettin' myself *pret*-ty drunk. I was high. So I said, 'I'm gonna shoot myself, man.'

"Duane said, 'How you gonna play the gig, man?'

"I said, 'I'll shoot myself in the foot.'

"He said, 'Hmm, that might work.'

"Duane started on thinking. He said, 'We'll have a party. We'll get real good and fucked up, we'll get a box, fill it with sawdust, put it in the garage, and take care of business. Right after that we'll put you in the car, take you to the hospital, and take you from the hospital straight to the induction center. We'll time it.'

"About three days passed. We had the party. A bunch of girls over there, a bunch of whiskey. I drank half a quart of whiskey. I was three sheets to the wind. I was about ready to shoot myself so I went out there. I came back in. I said, 'Duane, we forgot somethin'.' He said, 'What?'

" 'A fuckin' gun, Hal!'

"So we rode over to the 'other side of town,' as they referred to it back then, and said to the first black dude on the corner, 'Hey, man! I want to buy a pistol!'

" 'Man, what are you talkin' about?'

" 'We want to buy a .22 Saturday Night Special.'

"He said, 'I might be able to take care of that.'

" 'Good, how much is it?'

" 'How much you got?'

" 'Twenty-five dollars.'

" 'Well, that's how much it is.'

"So we got the gun and three bullets and went home. I was thinkin', 'Now I gotta *do* this.' Drunk as I was, I was still fixin' to shoot my own ass. I mean, this is gettin' serious. So I sat down and I was studyin' my foot chart. Here's the long bone and it comes to a V with the bone next to it. I figure I want to put the bullet right between 'em so I crack both but don't break either one. Let the bullet pass right through. Then I took a knife and carved a line down the nose of the bullet so it'd leave a little piece in there. 'Cause if you've got any metal in your body the army won't take you.

"I had a target drawn on my shoe. On my moccasin. I set my foot up there, took the pistol, cocked it back . . . and said, '*Oh, my God, what am I doin'*? Am I crazy? I'm about to shoot myself!'

"Pretty soon Duane comes in. 'Well, I didn't hear no noise. Goddamn, you gonna do it? Shit, boy, put up or shut up! We got all these people over here expectin' a foot-shootin' party!'

"I said, 'Look, man, you're talkin' about a bullet in my foot!'

"He said, 'I know, man. Don't worry about it. Come on. I'll shoot you.' "

Gregg imitated a drunken Duane picking up the gun, stumbling around, and accidentally pointing it between Gregg's eyes.

"I said, 'Wait! You're gonna miss and hit me in the fuckin' head!' So I went back in the house to drink some more whiskey and Duane followed, callin' me names and gettin' me madder till I said, 'Well, screw you, man!' "

"I grabbed that pistol, drew a bead on my foot, and *bam*! Flames shot out of that damn ol' cheap-ass pistol and scared me to death. I don't know where that propulsion came from, but I was straight up off the ground. Duane was out the door and caught me on the fly.

"For three seconds I thought I was dead. Three seconds. Then it numbed up to my thigh. I got in the damn car, wrapped a towel around it, and joked around on my way to the hospital. The first thing they did was give me morphine. Now I'm really fucked up.

"By now the leather from the moccasin had sunk into

the bullet hole. I looked at it and turned to my brother and said, 'Duane! There's a target drawn on my left shoe! They might just figure out what the hell we were up to!'

"Duane says, 'Oh, no!' But just then the doctor comes in and wheels me into the damn room. I thought, 'Oh, shit, now I'm goin' to jail for sure.' The doctor says, 'What have we got here? He rips the shoe right off, throws it behind him, and never recognizes the damn target. By this time Duane comes in and he's drawn a target on the other shoe!

"All the doctor did was stick a tube of what looked like Blistex in the hole, bandage it up, and sent me home. I got back outside with that big bandage on and said, 'Shit! The moccasins are still in there!' So Duane snuck back in the O.R. an' stole those shoes. How he got in there I'll never know.

"Duane took me to the induction center and they said, 'What the hell happened to you?' I said, 'Man, I was up in the attic looking through my gun collection when my favorite .22 magnum went off!' "

The limousine came to a halt and the chauffeur opened the door.

"It healed up later," Gregg sighed. "But by then I got off by being 'sole surviving son.' "

September 1990

STEVIE RAY VAUGHAN

BY TIMOTHY

WHITE

■

It was a kind of World Series of archival cutting contests. Stevie Ray Vaughan, hunched over his "sweetheart" ax, a chocolate brown '59 Stratocaster, sat in a semi-darkened Manhattan studio trading licks with the greatest heroes of yore. He swapped lacerating Robert Johnson–derived lines with Elmore James on "Goodbye Baby," merged growling riffs with Howlin' Wolf's lead guitarist Willie Johnson on "Moanin' at Midnight," barked out a shifting cadent blues alongside John Lee Hooker on

"Boogie Chillen," and huddled with Lightnin' Hopkins to share a tart Texas shuffle on "Gimme Back That Wig (I Bought You Babe, and Let Your Doggone Head Go Bald)."

Stevie Ray's musical cohorts were present in spirit courtesy of a vintage Kent Records compilation album called *Underground Blues*, but the fact that Vaughan could accompany these legends, duet-style, on a blink's notice, spoke volumes about the kind of artist—and appreciator— he surely was. This interview with Stevie Ray Vaughan took place in October 1989 at Sound on Sound Studios on West 45th Street in New York. The entire conversation unfolded with Vaughan's guitar cradled in his arms. The encyclopedic grasp he had of his heroes' myriad individual styles was further deepened by a unique tenderness toward their individual intentions. Stevie Ray was as understanding of the reasons *why* a person played the blues, the needs and desires behind the notes, as he was of the end results. A student of humanity, he also knew that it's the amateurs who usually make the most history by inventing their own place in it.

As the last strains of *Underground Blues* faded away, Stevie Ray looked up from his guitar, smiled broadly, and said, "Man, that album is a journey—just fantastic. You got any others like that here?" No, he was told, but he had *him* as a resource to continue the trek through the living musical heritage he so loved. This talk with the late, great Stevie Ray Vaughan is a moving reminder of how much we lost when we lost him, and how much he left behind for us to learn to appreciate.

MUSICIAN: *"Riviera Paradise" has a beautiful bittersweet quality. But no matter what you're playing, fast or slow, you never crowd your notes and phrases. Everything's rounded out, right on the dime. Is there a philosophy to that sort of attention to detail in your playing?*

S.R.V.: What I'm trying to do in those things is find that clarity, when I can let go of whatever it would be, ego or self-consciousness. Since I can't read music, I find I do the best when I just listen to where I'm trying to go with it and where it *can* go. And not try to rush it. Not try to make up things as I'm going, necessarily, but just let them come out. Then I'm a lot better off. If I start trying to pay attention to where I am on the neck and the proper way to do this or that, I end up thinking *that* thing through instead of playing from my heart. When I've played from my mind I get in trouble.

MUSICIAN: *There's a nice sense of intuition in your playing. It's the idea that you feel so close to your instrument, you're trying to think out loud with it.*

S.R.V.: I don't know if it's *think*, really, but just feel and express. I've spent many years married to these guitars, especially this one. . . . I found this one in '73, I believe, at a store in Austin. I had my first Stratocaster at about that time and I was having problems with the intonation and it was driving me nuts! I went to get it worked on, but as I walked up I saw this guitar just hanging there in the window and looking at me, and I was looking back. I walked straight up to the counter and handed the guy my guitar and said, "Will you trade me this guitar for that one over there?" He said, "Yes." And I said, "Even?" and he said, "Yeah," and I said, "Give it to me!" and I picked this one up and went and plugged it in and it sounded just like I wanted it to, just like I thought it would. It felt just perfect for me. Had it ever since.

MUSICIAN: *"Riviera Paradise" is like good brandy going down. How did you come to write it?*

S.R.V.: It's actually like an extension of the style of "Lenny," off the first album. Originally I came up with it about '84 and I was looking for those same qualities—there were some rough times going on at home. A lot of us go through really drastic up-and-down hardships between relationships, when we don't know really how to love someone right. "Lenny" was written to soothe, and "Riviera Paradise" comes from the same place. I wasn't wanting to just copy myself, I was wanting to go ahead and say something with the song and it was down to where I couldn't find the chords I needed, I started just sticking my hand on the neck, pushing my fingers down, and saying, "What's that sound like?" The song went through a lot of different meanings between '84 and now. Finally I got back to where I was coming from originally, which was looking for the willingness to make things right with the people that had been hurt in these relationships. That's really where it comes from.

MUSICIAN: *Yeah, it seems to come from a very humble, very compassionate place, wanting to build those bridges and keeping those bridges strong.*

S.R.V.: Yeah, building bridges instead of tearing them down, that's exactly what it's about.

MUSICIAN: *Your vocals on "Crossfire" were as strong and new as your playing had always been.*

S.R.V.: Well, thank you, man. The way I see it, it's a learning process every time I go in the studio, actually every time we do a gig or I'm just walking around the house or in the shower or whatever, trying to learn how to sing. I've always wanted to work that out. It's something that doesn't come quite so easily as guitar playing to me. And a lot of the direction that I've had has been of course through records and through contact with a lot of the people that I've really looked up to all my life. But a lot of it really goes to Doyle Bramhall, who I had the pleasure of writing a lot of songs with on *In Step*. I've known him since I was about eleven, twelve years old and always really liked the way he sang, and his influences were a lot of the same singers that were mine. Everybody from Ray Charles,

206

Bobby Bland, B. B. King, Howlin' Wolf, Muddy Waters. I've always liked how they sang and I've always liked how Doyle sang, but for me it's just taken a lot more work.

MUSICIAN: *It's interesting where you pick up these bits of inspiration both from people who are right there in the fabric of your own life, like Doyle, and from the old records. People might not realize that even old heroes of yours like Magic Sam learned to play the blues by listening to Muddy Waters and Little Walter records. So many people did that; even back to the earliest days when they were playing the oldest Robert Johnson 78s, that was a tradition.*

S.R.V.: Yeah, and you can also go and *see* the people. But by listening to the records you can sit at home and start it over, find where you're coming from. It's a real neat deal! And you can dress up like you want to in your room and nobody knows! [*laughter*]

MUSICIAN: *"Let Me Love You, Baby" is so focused, both Buddy Guy's famous 1963 live approach on* Folk Festival of the Blues *and your modern interpretation of it. His music obviously brings out a lot of spirit in you. It's a good place to build from because it's so direct.*

S.R.V.: It's the simple direct things that seem to get to the point, and it's not all polished over with overproduction or anything. I don't know what I would have done if I'd had to start off my learning process in music with so much production going on. I wouldn't have known what to do. I'm really glad that my crystal radio worked real well to get Ernie's Record Mart in Gallatin, Tennessee, and things like that! And back in the time when you'd hear B. B. King and Jimmy Reed and Buddy Guy, things like that on Top Forty radio, I was just real fortunate in that way.

MUSICIAN: *I know a big influence on Buddy Guy when he was coming up was T-Bone Walker. How would you contrast their approaches?*

S.R.V.: T-Bone was aggressive. Buddy can go from one

end of the spectrum to the other. He can play quieter than anybody I've ever heard. I play pretty loud a lot of times, but Buddy's tones are just incredible. But Buddy's style is not necessarily such a technical style, it's just more like raw meat in a lot of ways. A lot of his earlier records seem to be really toned down and to the point.

MUSICIAN: *Like "One Room Country Shack"?*

S.R.V.: Yeah! And part of the tone thing has to do with, the way he puts it, that he was *told* to turn down for those records—they wouldn't let him go crazy. [*laughter*] He may or may not like this, but from a guitar player's standpoint I'm really glad I got to hear him that way as well because he pulls so much emotion out of so little volume. Buddy's just got this cool feel to everything he does.

MUSICIAN: *He's got a real proud style, a strut quality.*

S.R.V.: Oh, yeah, and when he sings, it's just compounded. Girls fall over and sweat and die! Every once in a while I get the chance to go and play with Buddy and he gets me every time, because we could try to go to Mars on guitars but then he'd start singing, sing a couple of lines, and then stick the mike in front of me! What are you going to do? What is a person going to do? [*laughter*]

MUSICIAN: *Another tradition in the blues is cutting contests. Years ago at Chicago's Blue Flame Club, Buddy Guy walked off the street and Otis Rush and Magic Sam were there and he just got up and played in what was essentially their style! That was the beginning of his reputation in Chicago. Have you ever had the chance to get together with Buddy in this kind of cutting contest?*

S.R.V.: Yeah! Not too long ago I got to do it at his new club, Legends, in Chicago, and before that it's been times at the Lone Star in New York City or at various different Antone's—it's moved several times—around Austin; and we've gotten to do it at the Chicago Blues Festival quite a few years ago. Every time I get to run into Buddy that's pretty much what we end up doing. We go for the throat, and I just love it! But then he always starts singing again [*laughs*] and then it's all over, you know?

MUSICIAN: *Was your first guitar the Gibson Messenger you got in '63?*

S.R.V.: That was my first electric, yeah. That was Jimmie's first electric as well, and he just handed it down when he got a 330 and later on he probably changed to Les Pauls and Telecasters. Gave me a '51 Tele, a cross between a Broadcaster and a Tele that I rebuilt and ended up letting someone talk me into selling and I'm still kicking myself! Still looking for it, by the way! So if somebody finds a guitar that says "Jimbo" on the back and it's the right one, it's a real deal—you can come *rape* me for it, or my pocketbook anyway!

MUSICIAN: *Do you recall the first song that you worked out on electric guitar? Maybe that '51 Tele?*

S.R.V.: A lot of the stuff I was learning early on had to do with Jimmy Reed kind of things. Early on Jimmie and I did learn something that I ended up playing with Dick Dale not long ago.

MUSICIAN: *Dick Dale from the Del-Tones, the surf-guitar king?*

S.R.V.: [*Plays some surf guitar lines*] Yeah, those things were popular then, but it was just a lot of fun to learn that stuff—Ray Sharp and the Razor Blades. It's the real simple things, you know? Then of course the Beatles came out and we heard about the Bluesbreakers, and at the same time we were starting to hear about Muddy Waters and Howlin' Wolf, Buddy Guy, B. B. King, Freddie King, and Lonnie Mack, and on and on. *Wham* [Lonnie Mack's album *The Wham of That Memphis Man*] was the first record I bought. Somebody was in the right corner upstairs on that one 'cause I finally ended up getting the chance to work with Lonnie. Things like "Why" still kill me. And then on

Lonnie's *Strike Like Lightning*, the song "Stop" was just a killer. Nobody can play a wang-bar like that.

And then along came Albert King records. It's funny, because when I was about twelve I had been a dishwasher for a while and part of my job was to clean out the trash bin. That involved standing on these big fifty-five-gallon barrels with wooden lids on them, where they'd put all the hot grease. And one day I was out there cleaning out the bin, having a blast, and the top broke and I fell in. Just as I finally got out—I'd been up to about my chest in grease—they came with two fresh hot vats of boiling grease and I got out just in time. If I'd taken a break later, I would have been a fried guy! The woman fired me because I broke the lids on the barrel and right then and there I decided, "Wait a minute, this is not what I want to do. I want to play guitar like Albert King!" And that's the last job I've had other than playing guitar. So thank you, Albert, for helping me there. [*laughs*]

MUSICIAN: *Talking about Albert and B. B. King and these kind of high, bent-string, single-note lines—a song on Soul to Soul,* "Ain't Gonna Give Up on Love," *has a bit of that flavor.*

S.R.V.: Some of my favorite stuff, man, is to play Albert King things and be able to do 'em in 1989 or whatever, 2010! I hope that style of music and the reality of blues—everybody goes through those ups and downs—never leaves our music. I hope we don't decide as a mass to get rid of all the real things and just put in the synthetic hypnotic music and leave those things alone. I hope that *never* happens.

MUSICIAN: *Let's go through a little personal history and weave a little Texas blues history into it. You're the second son of Jimmy Lee and Martha Vaughan and you grew up in the Oak Cliff section of Dallas. What is the Oak Cliff area like?*

S.R.V.: It's not like J.R.'s joint! It's more of a down-home neighborhood. It was actually another town separate from Dallas for many, many years and Dallas grew around it. In another part of Oak Cliff, across the tracks I suppose, was where T-Bone Walker was from, and Leadbelly. All these people were from there: Charlie Christian, Freddie King. Oak Cliff was a breeding ground for a lot of music, lots of culture that's been torn down to make room for sky-risers.

MUSICIAN: *What was your first instrument?*

S.R.V.: My first instrument was shoe boxes and pie pans, with clothes hangers for sticks. And then it was when Jimmie got a guitar, my parents got me a lap steel which I had *no* idea what to do with. And then I got an acoustic guitar, one of those little Roy Rogers models made out of Masonite, and it wouldn't tune, so we took half the strings off and struck it more like a bass and tuned it down. Jimmie kept playing his guitar—I believe it was an Airline box acoustic—and over the years I kept trying to fool around with drums here and there.

Jimmie plays drums better than I could. He's one of those guys who, when he picks anything up, it just sounds right, you know? And it doesn't look like he's doing *any-thing!* [*laughs*] He kept on playing guitar and picked up several types of instruments, everything from steel guitars to cornet, fiddle, '51 Chevys—*and* he's a great bass player. I played bass for a while in Jimmy's band called the Texas Storm. It was just a few months, but I learned a lot there, mainly steel guitar, little bit of drums.

MUSICIAN: *You were about ten when you were in a group called the Shantones, and then in junior high you were in a group called Blackbird. What did those bands sound like?*

S.R.V.: Well, in the Shantones we thought we had a band and we finally played a talent show and realized in the middle of our song that we didn't know the whole thing. [*laughs*] We weren't together very long! We went through different bands and really started learning what was going on. Blackbird went through so many different people, like one of the springboard deals: I learned how to play with someone until the energy was gone and before it was really a deadbeat kind of thing, we would have the sense enough to go ahead and change members so we could keep fresh. It was a real neat growing experience.

Blackbird ended up moving to Austin New Year's Eve of '72. It was great. We decided to move there on the *way* there and I moved into a club called Rolling Hills that a friend of mine owned. I slept on the pool table, the stage, the floor, whatever the weather permitted. And to tell you the truth, it was some of my favorite times. I didn't have a dime, but who cares? I was doing what I wanted and was around people I wanted to be around and it was *always* good music. A lot of other bands had gone to Austin because in Austin you could play what you wanted and that was all there was to it. You didn't have to go by some club owner's idea of what you ought to sound like or play this list of songs that he handed you. You might as well have had a quarter slot in your ear, you know? The whole scene in Austin was when someone needed a fresh bit of energy in their band—kind of like every three to six months, something like that—all the bands would just shuffle the cards of players. Everybody learned a whole lot, and eventually everybody found slots with other musicians that they really wanted to stay with.

MUSICIAN: *You were roughly seventeen or so in '72. Wasn't it a little on the cold side that winter in Austin?*

S.R.V.: Yeah, it didn't bother me, though. I don't know. I don't think that I really want to lose everything right now, but it was a real neat thing for me, a real growing experience, and it's something I never could regret.

MUSICIAN: *People know Austin as a place where rock and country kind of got together in the Sixties, places like*

212

Threadgill's Bar, Armadillo World Headquarters. But there's also a real rich blues and R&B tradition coming out of that town, a lot happening in the R&B bars on Sixth Street.

S.R.V.: There always has been. W. C. Clark's one of the people who's been involved in that for years and years, as well as the Jets and Bill Campbell. There was a real rich deal. Like you said, it's been going on for years and years before I knew about it, obviously, but that's where Jimmie had moved, probably late Sixties, I guess, maybe as late as '70. He had been involved with a lot of that. It's still going on there. There's a new phase of it, a lot of young kids growing up and doing the same thing. Now, Sixth Street, even though it can be a little bit, uh . . . I don't know . . . it seemed as if it was going to turn into more than a Bourbon Street and get out of hand for a while. But now it seems there's a lot of clubs lining Sixth Street and you can just walk up and down the street and hear all kinds of young cats playing what they're really trying to find home with. It's happening all again. It's a great thing. But in Dallas blues clubs like the Cellar, if you were black you could not get in! Thank God we got to get out of Dallas and go down to Austin, where that whole hypocritical deal wasn't so evident.

MUSICIAN: *Was there any song that you put together in those early years that turned up on one of your albums later?*

S.R.V.: "Pride and Joy" was kind of funny. I'd written the song in the studio, recorded it right then, and brought it home to the girlfriend that I'd had at the time. I don't know what the problem was, but she didn't think it was really about her and we got into this big argument, so I got back in the car and went back into the studio and rewrote some of the words to the song—I'm crying for the demo where I'd put these different words over the same track— and brought this home and went, "Here." [*laughter*]

MUSICIAN: *Songs While-U-Wait!*

S.R.V.: Songs While-U-Wait—you got it! I'm glad to say it ended up going back to the original version. [*laughter*]

MUSICIAN: *"Rude Mood," another song from* Texas Flood, *is like a crash course in modern Texas guitar technique. It's got fast shuffles on it, tight picking, those slippery chord combinations. If someone wanted to get the whole textbook in one place, or at least a good chunk of it, that would be a good song to start.*

S.R.V.: Well, it's actually like an extension of something I'd heard years and years ago of Lightnin' Hopkins called "Lightnin' Skyhop," and it's just me trying to not only remember what I'd learned from his styles, but to carry that on and take the song further. It's faster and it's got a few more tricks in it and this and that, but it's basically a takeoff of that song.

MUSICIAN: *Jimi Hendrix is obviously a hero of yours. You've kind of embraced his style but found new applications for it.*

S.R.V.: Well, his tone, his touch, his application of chords, his rhythms, his taking the idea of blues songs and turning them into modern-day things. Like "Manic Depression"—to him, that was a modern blues song even though it was a waltz [*starts strumming languid, moody Hendrix-type chords*]. That's pretty inventive kind of stuff to me, and the way he used a wang-bar was completely different than anybody I had heard do it. His soft, clear touch, you know. . . .

MUSICIAN: *It was a very tender touch that wasn't happening in rock 'n' roll, certainly not at that point in the Sixties.*

S.R.V.: And I believe he took tones a lot further than anyone had. If he couldn't get it out of a straight guitar, he would find an effect. I think he opened up all of those doors. For instance, the use of what's called an Octavia. He opened all those doors by being able to tell someone what he wanted and making use of fuzzes. What he ended up

214

doing with all that was the same thing that people go for. Listen to "The Star Spangled Banner"—if that's not where people got the idea to try and go for synthesizer sounds, I'm not sure where it would be from. Imagine what that's opened up for everyone! I think he just continued to try and take things further and he wasn't afraid of talking about spiritual things in his songs and trying to grow. Even though we sometimes defeat our own purposes by our life-styles, or the different myths that we believe. . . . Like his dying because of drugs—some people think he was trying to. I think it was a mishap that happens to some of us when we get up in that whole deal. But it's obvious to me that he was trying to grow spiritually, and I think that was a new thing in rock music. He stretched all the boundaries.

MUSICIAN: *There's a wonderful song on* Soul to Soul *called "Say What" that's got really eloquent wah-wah work in it. There's a nice shading of Hendrix inspiration in it.*

S.R.V.: Well, it was definitely inspired by him. If you listen to a lot of his stuff, you could hear the roots coming, a lot of the sounds sounded old and brand-new at the same time. The emotions seem to be not dated at all. And I think that's what he was tapping into as well when he headed off into jazz areas, and what he was trying to do toward the end. I say "at the end"—who can call it that? I get the idea that all he experienced is kind of like what fusion's supposed to be, you know? I mean, he seemed to not only play guitar on guitar, but he played *everything* on guitar. I don't know what else to call it. He just played music. No matter how many walls he knocked down to get there.

MUSICIAN: *Let's talk about Texas R&B and blues, about Texas music as you experienced it. The backbone of Texas music is the blues shuffle.*

S.R.V.: One of my favorites has always been [*starts playing some shuffles*] Freddie King's "Hideaway," things like that. Albert Collins' "Don't Lose Your Cool." A lot of music that came out in years gone by, I don't know that it's so much this way now, but it seems to me that music used to be more based on common everyday occurrences, like a train sound going down the track, someone walking down the street, things like that. A horse walking, you know? That's where these rhythms came from.

MUSICIAN: *People take this stuff from life. Jimi Hendrix used to say he got some of those sounds from his days as a paratrooper: The door of that plane would fly open and whoooooshh, and he'd go, "Whoa, let me think of a sound that makes me feel the way I feel right now before I jump." And in listening to you play those various shuffles, there's such a hopeful sound to it. It's like, "What's next? I'm ready for whatever comes around the corner." Such a thing of optimism in those great Texas shuffles.*

S.R.V.: Even though Texas music in a lot of ways is rough-and-tumble, it also seems to me to be about feeling better. Like there's always a good time in it. Even if it's a real down blues tune. Albert King described something to me one time that really made a lot of sense: No matter whether it's a real down song about everything going wrong or whether it's the upside of it—found something new or got it together with my woman, or whatever—it's all to soothe, the blues is all to soothe. Whether you got to get mad first or you've already been mad, it's all to *soothe*. And I think that's one thing that a lot of people miss about blues.

MUSICIAN: *One of my favorite songs from* Couldn't Stand the Weather *is "Scuttle Buttin'." There's so much energy! How did that come about?*

S.R.V.: Actually, that's me trying to say thank you to Lonnie Mack, basically. "Scuttle Buttin' " came out of me trying to figure out how to play "Chicken Pickin'." [*laughs*] It wasn't like I was just trying to steal him blind or anything, it was just like me kind of trying to say thank you. And we ended up doing it a lot of times if we got to run into each other.

MUSICIAN: *People may know the name of your band comes from the great Otis Rush song, "Double Trouble." Otis is from Philadelphia, Mississippi, but is best known as one of the kingpins of the postwar Chicago blues sound. It's interesting how Texas and Chicago have shaken hands in so many ways in your music.*

S.R.V.: You know, the tie between Texas, Louisiana, and Chicago, all those areas had a lot to do with train lines, railroad tracks, and I think there was always a lot closer connection than a lot of us realized. Because it was always a migratory route. Freddie King made it in Chicago in a lot of ways. The two styles of music are a little bit different, but these days it's a lot more intertwined, and I'm really glad I've gotten to know a lot of those people, like Otis Rush, Buddy Guy, gotten a chance to play with them. I don't think I've seen anyone caress a guitar and hug it and play it like Otis Rush. And then he opens his mouth. He's another one of those people who opens his mouth and you just . . . shudder. . . . Because it's so to the bone. [*starts playing "I Can't Quit You" and singing*] I'm glad I remembered the words! [*laughs*]

MUSICIAN: *How did you record Stevie Wonder's "Superstition?"*

S.R.V.: One day while we were rehearsing for the *Live Alive* album we started playing around with "Superstition" and one of the crew members got all excited and said, "If y'all do that song it'd be a hit." It felt real good and two or three days later we recorded it. And then as we were trying to find the right mixing studio, a friend of mine told me that we ought to just call Stevie, call up Wonderland and say, "Hey, man, I'm a fan of yours and really looking for a studio. . . . Is yours available?" We finally did and it was just incredible. They welcomed us in, gave us a better rate

217

than anybody else around, treated us well, gave us the studio for twenty-four hours a day. I had met him at the Grammys or wherever, different places over the years, and all of a sudden I would get these great phone calls in the middle of the night. Imagine this: being dead asleep, picking up the phone, and Stevie Wonder is singing to you! Making it up as he goes! It's continued like that and I finally got the chance to play on one of his records. There's nobody like the man—to just sit there and watch him write these things on the spot. And the funny thing is he'll do this while carrying on a conversation on two different phones and with a couple of people in the room, while he's playing a couple of different keyboards as well. Plus he's programming his computer to play the song that he's fixing to play in a few minutes! And he's doing all this at the same time, cognizant of everything going on. You get up and start to tiptoe out of the room and he goes, "Where you going?" It's like, who needs eyes, you know? And he's so full of love and so full of truth, it's a real neat thing.

MUSICIAN: *You've played with Jeff Beck, too. Is there a Jeff Beck song that you've played over the years, in a band here, a band there?*

S.R.V.: *[starts playing "Guitar Boogie"]* This was actually a Chuck Berry song that Jeff took and redid, called it "Jeff's Boogie." All the gunslingers in the world had six strings on their guns. Every time you'd walk into a club like the Cellar, if somebody new walked in, it was like time for everybody to pull out their gunslinging material, and everybody would play "Jeff's Boogie." You'd play it part of the way, then double-time it and double-time it again. It was just kind of a staple of what I grew up with. *[Starts playing "Jeff's Boogie"]* Actually, Chuck Berry's version was a lot more tame, but Jeff Beck took it and had *wild* guitars and echo and the whole bit. He's another one of those guys that could play incredibly beautiful and incredibly . . . just mean, you know?

MUSICIAN: *Like an explosion.*

S.R.V.: Yeah! Very much. And he can play some of the weirdest stuff I've ever heard and make it completely work. I don't know whether he's riding a wave or if he can think that quick to think it out first, but it doesn't really matter, you know? Incredible.

MUSICIAN: *There's a lot of personal wisdom in "Wall of Denial."*

S.R.V.: The musical part of it started off as me just trying to find a new way to play a 6/8 kind of a feel. The more I played with it, the more I started looking for something I could use lyrically that really *meant* something, instead of just . . . "got a new car" or "got a lot of money in the bank"—who cares? I started looking through lyrics that I'd come up with and ideas that I'd found that had really helped me in my life, and pulled these pieces and parts together. Not necessarily in a song form, but as pieces and parts of something that could grow. Doyle and I went over the thing at one of our get-togethers, which was basically he and I would sit down and talk about what was going on in our lives for a few hours and boil it down to the real and what we could use—we would write it down. I pulled out these pieces and parts of songs that I'd had, or just ideas that we had written out but not tied together, and a lot of the things we came up with were things that were really helping us. We would just insert them and the whole thing would start coming together and there'd be a song. We didn't have a title. Doyle was driving home, pulled out his little pencil, and just wrote "Wall of Denial" on top of the piece of paper. And he came back and said that to me. I was talking to my manager on the phone and telling him what-all we'd gotten done and what we were going to work on next. I said, "Well, I think we're going to work on . . ." All of a sudden Doyle goes, "A wall of deniyalllllllll . . ." and I went, "I'll see you later," hung the phone up, turned around, and said, "What?" And we went from there, started the very first part of the song, and I pulled it out and said, "Here's the first verse—you got the chords." And then we got back to the "wall of denial" part and put in the second verse and it all fell together just like that.

MUSICIAN: *There's a really beautiful couplet in there: "We're never safe from the truth, but in the truth we can survive."*

S.R.V.: That's something I learned just looking, you know, *looking* for things that really could help me, and just *anyone*, in recovery with addiction and drugs. The idea is out of a real spiritual book called *The Course* that's been real helpful to a lot of people. The principle is just as plain as it can be: We always—well, many times—try to hide from the truth, thinking we can; that we'll be safe by covering something up when in fact if you try to cover up those things that really are too hard to look at, they end up coming out like razor blades or explosions in our lives and tear things up. And the sooner we can learn to go back to the truth we'll be a lot better off; then it sets us free.

June 1991

EARL PALMER

THE RHYTHM BOMBER,

THE FUNK MACHINE

FROM NEW ORLEANS

BY TONY SCHERMAN

■

Right over there my mother had her dancing group, the Rinky Dinks Revue. Over here was a sandwich place called Joe Sheep's, they had the best hot sausage sandwiches in town for a dime. Joe Sheep was an old guy, light-complected guy, and he was the meanest old so-and-so you ever met. You'd come up there to get a sandwich: 'Whatcha want, li'l nigger?' 'I wanna hot sausage sandwich.' You goin' through your pockets, pullin' pennies out: 'Hurry up, you little mother-

fucker!' Oh, he was a terrible old man, but those sandwiches was delicious!"

The rental car came up St. Philip Street, past a group
of poker-faced stoopsitters. Interrupting his travelogue, the
driver, a handsome gravelly-voiced man in a tan summer
suit, rolled down his window.

"Hey! Any y'all seen Bo' Weevil?"

"Naw, man."

"Well, tell him his cousin Earl said hello."

"Earl Palmer?" Three pairs of eyes widened.

"Yeah, man, how y'all doin'?" The driver confided to
his carmate: "Bo' Weevil—that's my cousin Arthur
Landry." The father of rock 'n' roll drumming was taking
a sentimental drive, with many stops, through the neighborhood where he'd spent his first thirty years, the Treme
(pronounced Tre-*may*) section of New Orleans. He pulled
up across from a tumbledown wooden building with a
mansard roof and lettering right across its faded-green
slats: "Caldonia Bar." "This the new Caldonia," said Earl,
climbing out with a groan. "Ol' Caldonia was back where
Armstrong Park is now; Professor Longhair used to play
there for wine, for nothin'." From the honky-tonk came
raucous cries and jukebox noise: the ReBirth Brass Band's
"Do Whatcha Wanna," B. B. King. Earl paused to admire a
sturdy local, about eighteen months old. "How ya doin',
little man, little man, want some candy, man?" A nice little
compact rolled up, a friendly-faced kid at the wheel. "Hey!"
someone said. "That's Kermit from the ReBirth Brass
Band!" An old man pointed at Earl. "Hey! This is Earl
Palmer!" The kid's face lit up and he stopped. A little awk-
wardly, Earl sauntered up to the car, spat over his shoulder.
They hadn't much to say, it was just the mutual attraction
of the famous: an authentic local hero, sixty-seven years
old, and a youngblood on his first pretty car. "We playin'
at Armstrong Park, five-thirty tonight," said Kermit, "c'mon

down if you like." "Okay, bruh," said Earl, "y'all have a nice time."

A quick beer and Earl was ready to roll. "Over there," he said, "is Craig Elementary. The [Count Basie] trombonist Bennie Powell grew up across the street"—second floor of a rundown building facing the brick school—"and he would play hooky, hang out that window right there makin' faces at us in the geography room. We're goin', 'Miz Gair, Miz Gair! Bennie's not sick, lookit him!' and he'd duck. Soon as she turned around he'd pop up, stick his tongue out."

Earl Palmer has his own way of driving, in which signals do not figure prominently. He sped through the French Quarter, turned right onto Canal, and screeched to a stop. "Aw, Jesus god*damn*, I shoulda went toward the river. I was thinking we were headed to Steve's." He pulled a swashbuckling U-turn. "Steve Angrum is a very, very close friend of mine. He's a bitchin' piano player, man, he was *smaaart* in music school, but he's so lazy! His sister Alice was married at one time to Snookum Russell, who had a great touring band, great musician, but if you saw his face you'd know why they called him Snookum, he was the ugliest little sonofabitch you ever seen. Looked just like a fish. He worked in the French Quarter for years, terrific piano player, great arranger, and a hell of a good singer, too. But he was ugly."

Earl was in town for the annual Jazz & Heritage Festival (and to buy the hot sausage he freezes and brings back home to L.A.). After thirty-five years in California, his voice still has a slight Creole lilt; "tomtom" is almost "tumtum." "Last night," he said, "I went to hear Nicholas Payton. *Awesome* seventeen-year-old trumpeter. Seventeen—I got drawers that old! I think I'm wearing a pair today! A friend of mine heard Payton; she was furious 'cause Art Blakey drowned him out. She said, 'Jesus Christ, he oughta know how to play the drums by now.' I said, 'Give him a break, he's seventy-five and deaf.' You have to understand one thing, you're dealing with a bunch of guys who dissipated for seventy years. Very big dissipators. Particularly Blakey.

"Anyway, who cares if a drummer is loud? I love Tony Williams, man. Once you understand he's loud, you listen to what he's playin', not how loud; you evaluate the performance, not the volume. Tony is a fantastic drummer. There's a younger guy that's pretty awesome, not as a jazz player but overall, and that's Dave Weckl. The other guy is Smitty Smith. Smitty-oh, brother! Ohhh! *Oy vey!*"

"What kind of player do you think you'd have become if you hadn't gotten so involved in the studio?"

"A good player, but just another good player. Gettin' involved in the studio in that exacting way, that's what made me a really confident player. When you walk away from a difficult session, or a film, some bastard of a part, knowing the music was hard and you played it perfectly and the thirty-fifth take sounded like you *loved* it, that's when you know, 'I've arrived, I'm a *musician.*' Not a soloist—you wanna be a soloist, get your own band.

" 'Cause the drums are not a lead instrument." Earl suddenly burst out laughing. "Except this one time, way up in the mountains outside L.A., this party where none of the guys could play. The leader kept saying, 'If you don't know the song, lay out!' I ended up playing by myself! Don't ever let anyone tell you the drums can't play the melody!" Earl was almost weeping with laughter. " 'Lay out! Lay out!' I was playin' alone!"

"So who's your favorite drummer?"

"All-time? Buddy Rich. Buddy Rich is a freak, man, he was born a fuckin' drum. But he'd try to goad people into fightin' him, which nobody would because he was a great fighter. Small but tenacious, man. Mean. Could fight.

"I also idolized Shelly Manne. I first met him right here

in 1951. I waited for him after a concert. The cop kept saying, 'Get back, boy.' Shelly came out and turned to go the other way, so I started after him, saying 'Hey, Shelly!' The cop grabbed me. 'Nigger, didn't I tell you to get back?' Shelly heard that, turned around, and said, 'Oh, there you are, I was waiting for you!' He had never seen me in his life. Later he stuck his neck out to get me gigs. I ended up naming my daughter after him."

In a sandwich shop in Metairie, Earl sat down to a big oyster po' boy. Watching Earl Palmer leaf through *Musician* is unsettling: On page after page are artists he's worked with. Elvis Costello on *King of America* ("Ray Brown and I thought he was kinda uppity until T-Bone Burnett said, 'No, man, he's in awe.' 'Awe? He's a millionaire and we ain't got a fuckin' quarter!' "). Bonnie Raitt ("I knew her father, too; we used to have a few drinks at Donte's"). "The Old Laughing Lady" on Neil Young's classic first album. Tina Turner, Frank Sinatra, Sarah Vaughan (*The Explosive Side of Sarah Vaughan* has some of Earl's finest big-band/jazz work), John Lee Hooker. Not to mention hundreds of others: Ritchie Valens ("La Bamba" and "Donna"), Ricky Nelson, Sam Cooke ("Shake," "You Send Me," "Having a Party," "Twistin' the Night Away," "Wonderful World"), Eddie Cochran, Gene McDaniels ("100 Pounds of Clay"), the Righteous Brothers ("You've Lost That Lovin' Feelin'"), Lightnin' Hopkins, and Count Basie (on *Manufacturers of Soul*, a 1968 Basie collaboration with, amazingly, Jackie Wilson). Quincy Jones's music to *The Pawnbroker*, *In Cold Blood*, and *Rosemary's Baby* and hundreds of other movie scores—*Valley of the Dolls*, *Lady Sings the Blues*, *The Fabulous Baker Boys*, *The Hot Spot* (Earl's only Grammy nomination). Lalo Schifrin's cool "Mission Impossible" theme and Hale Curtin's bumptious "Meet the Flintstones"; the theme songs and incidental music to "77 Sunset Strip," "The Odd Couple," "Ironside."

Brenda Holloway (the original "You've Made Me So Very Happy"), Dobie Gray's "The In Crowd," the drum-thunder behind Ray Charles on "I Don't Need No Doctor," the whispers behind Ray on "I Can't Stop Loving You," *Diana Ross and the Supremes Join the Temptations*, Maria Muldaur's *Waitress in a Donut Shop*, Lou Rawls's "Dead End Street," Henry Mancini. Earl even played country—Buck Owens, Speedy West, Roy Clark's first demo. And all this came *after* the seven hectic years in New Orleans when Earl stitched the fibers of rock drumming.

With his angular cheekbones and wolfish gray-brown eyes, Earl is the product of a typically complicated black New Orleans lineage: French/Greek on his mother's side, Choctaw on his father's. Thelma Theophile was a nineteen-year-old tap dancer when she married Edward Palmer, a ship's cook from White Plains, New York. She was seven months pregnant when Edward Palmer was killed in a storm off Newfoundland. Thelma went home, and her only baby was born in 1924 in his grandma's house on Bienville Street.

By the age of five Earl was a professional dancer, working Bourbon Street sidewalks, speakeasies, and whorehouses in a white tux his mother had sewn. "We had a four-man troupe called Hats, Coats, Pants, and Buttons. These two guys named McElroy and Green, they were great dancers but they were junkies, they saw me and figured, 'Great! Little kid like that, he'll get plenty of tips we can steal.' But Pleasant Joseph joined us as the musical accompaniment on ukelele and he'd keep them other guys from stealin' my money. Put me on his back and carried me home at four in the morning, asleep." Pleasant Joseph became the blues singer Cousin Joe, and as an old man told an interviewer, "Earl Palmer was about nine or ten years old, but he was one of the greatest tap dancers in the city. He could outdance us all."

Eight or so months a year, Earl joined his mother on the TOBA black vaudeville circuit (the Theatre Owners Booking Agency, called by its artists "Tough on Black Asses"), playing segregated theaters with blues singer Ida Cox's Darktown Scandals. "It was the most marvelous life a kid could ask for": sharing the road with characters like Jazzlips Richardson, a minstrel-show dancer who flickered briefly on Broadway, Cox's husband Jesse Crump, a fine blues pianist from Paris, Texas. Earl met Satchel Paige, Josh Gibson, Bessie Smith; "I remember Miss Bessie bein' juiced, but everyone was juiced 'round then. . . . We traveled by bus and I'd sleep in the luggage rack. We'd get into town, daybreak in the mornin', and to keep from renting a room everybody slept on the big thick carpets in the theater lobby. But I'd go watch the matinee movie or go out on the town lookin' to meet the kids, foragin' around, playin'. Havin' a great time. I got asked to audition for Farina in the touring show of *Little Rascals*; my grandmother took me down and they said, 'The kid is fantastic but we can't use him.' 'Why not?' 'He's too light.' They thought about blackening my face, but my grandma said, 'They ain't puttin' no burnt cork on your face, you black enough, too black as it is.'

"Music didn't mean that much to me; it was mostly something useful to dance to. But when I started playing, I found I'd already gotten a whole musical education. As a tap dancer I already knew how to support a lyric. I'd learned the thirty-two-bar song form: where the bridge is, when to change colors. You'd do one step for eight bars, another for eight bars, then in the bridge you did a third step that was a little difficult and in the last eight you did your big, your hardest step." Not only did he know song structure, he came to drumming with a mental encyclopedia of rhythms and beats. "Tap dancing, after all, is only playing drums with your feet.

"So I'd started in on drums just after '45, when I came out of the service, and got kinda well known in town, though I didn't read or anything, didn't really know what I was doing." His buddy Red Tyler talked him into attending the Grunewald School of Music, a sort of vocational school that became a postwar haven for young jazzmen; Earl majored in piano, minored in percussion. The best bandleader in New Orleans was a hard-nosed trumpet player named Dave Bartholomew. "Dave's drummer was Dave Oxley, whose wife had been on the show with my mother; I called her 'Aunt Bernice'—I called all the ladies who'd been on the show 'Aunt.' Dave Oxley got into an argument with Bartholomew, who asked me to join the band. I said, 'I can't do that, my Uncle Dave's in the band.' 'No he ain't, I just fired him.' I called Uncle Dave and he said, 'You go ahead on, go ahead on, I ain't never goin' back to work for that so-and-so.' "

By 1949 Earl had played on his first hit, Bartholomew's proto-R&B "Country Boy," and almost from then on Earl Palmer's life split in two. If he became a legend as rock's first great drummer, he always considered himself something else. "I'm a jazz drummer, man. People forget—us guys on those Little Richard records were playing *jazz* before we played rhythm and blues. There wasn't any rhythm and blues! We were just able to adapt, make things a little funky, play a shuffle instead of a jazz feel—which is how rhythm and blues, rock 'n' roll, whatever you call it, came about. People *called* it rhythm and blues; I just called it doing the job.

"But my happiest times were playing jazz, trying out them Bird arrangements down at the Dew Drop." Hub of New Orleans' vibrant early-1950s jazz scene, the Dew Drop Inn was an amazing club/flophouse/de facto hiring hall, open twenty-four hours a day. R&B stars like Charles Brown would headline, and then everybody jammed until daybreak. "Cleanhead Vinson, Gene Ammons, Sonny Stitt. Bird himself, man. Charlie Parker was always losing rental cars, he would forget where he parked 'em, leave 'em all over town. I jammed with Bird with Jack Lamont, li'l alto player we had got killed by a bus." There was at least one job with Papa Celestin's old-time jazzers "in Baton Rouge, no, I think it was Biloxi. I tried to drink like them old guys and fell right off the stand." He even played with Armstrong, when Pops came home for 1949's Mardi Gras. "Dave Bartholomew's band played the New Orleans Coliseum and Pops was there. Earl Hines, too. Hines was an asshole, he said to Pops, 'You shouldn't be playing with those guys.' Pops said, 'Fuck ya, I'm home.' "

Rock 'n' roll, meanwhile, paid Earl's way: $41.25 for three hours or four songs, whichever came first, no overtime. As big-city record men moved in on New Orleans, what had started as a mere Forties continuation of the race-music recording trips of the Twenties and Thirties became rock's first great session scene, built around the "Studio Band" at tiny J&M Studios: Lee Allen and Red Tyler on saxophones, four or five key guitarists and pianists, Frank Fields on bass, and Earl Palmer, drums. From 1949 to 1957, Earl powered Fats Domino hits from "The Fat Man" to "I'm Walkin' " (Earl's favorite drum part from his New Orleans period, with its joyful snare/bass-drum parade beat). Three years after Earl put a stately, basically pre-rock shuffle on Lloyd Price's 1952 "Lawdy Miss Clawdy," an androgynous young screamer was brought to J&M, and Earl played on every big hit Little Richard would ever have (except "Keep a Knockin' " and "Ooh My Soul"): "Tutti Frutti," "Long Tall Sally," "Slippin' and Slidin'," "Rip It Up," "Lucille," "Jenny, Jenny," "Good Golly, Miss Molly." It may be Earl's greatest recorded legacy.

Married since 1947, Earl fell in love with Susan Weidenpesch, a white New Yorker, in 1956. Interracial marriage was illegal in Louisiana until the early Sixties (so was interracial music-making; Earl was busted for playing with whites in 1953), so in February 1957 Earl took a job as an A&R man with Aladdin Records and left for Los Angeles. He and Susan married in 1956; Susan died of cancer seven years later.

Had he never played a lick in California, Earl's place in pop music history would be safe. But he plunged into a huge body of work: by rough estimate, more than eleven thousand sessions by the early Eighties, upwards of twenty-five thousand pieces of music. Union scale was $60 a session; by the early Sixties Earl was getting double scale. His peak years were the late Sixties, when he cleared $180,000 a year, sometimes staying in the studio from nine A.M. until eleven P.M.: three three-hour sessions "and maybe I'd do a jingle in between. There were times we'd cut an album a day: six songs in the morning, six after lunch. We'd do an album with Gene McDaniels, next day one with Vicki Carr, next day the Crickets." Years of rim-shots gave Earl a carpenter's injury, a bad blood clot at the base of his left thumb.

"The first time I heard Earl," says drummer Jim Keltner, a member of the L.A. studio generation after Earl's, "was a Little Richard session at MGM. The power, groove, and taste—God, I thought, that feels so good! He had a mysterious sophistication so different from the rock drumming I knew at the time, the Sandy Nelson or Frankie Avalon records I'd heard. It was the way he could bring the sound out of the drums. Earl came up in an era when there were no drum mikes for live playing, or maybe just one, so he learned how to play loud, soft, and in-between. It's almost a lost art in today's rock 'n' roll."

The studios of L.A.—Gold Star, Sunset Sound, Radio Recorders, Western—were the main lab for the most profitable experiment ever in pop music: the bleaching of

R&B into rock 'n' roll, turning the salacious winks and nods of ghetto life into teen dreams, desexualizing "Work with Me Annie" into "Dance with Me Henry," "Sweet Little Sixteen" into "Surfin' USA." Earl was right there in the crucible. "If any single musician," wrote critic Robert Palmer recently, "can be credited with defining rock & roll as a rhythmic idiom distinct from the jump, R&B and all else that preceded it, that musician is surely Earl Palmer." By the time Earl left New Orleans, he'd already forged the new style, ironing the blues shuffle into a straight 4/4 with a heavy backbeat and a peppery, syncopated bass drum straight from New Orleans parade bands. Earl was better than first-rate: He was a creator.

In the Great Experiment, the nuttiest professor of all was Phil Spector, who made a point of calling rock 'n' roll "pop blues" and used a bedrock of R&B (and mostly black artists) to build huge, neo-Romantic cathedrals of sound for America's teenagers: "little symphonies for the kids," as he put it. Spector's first-call drummer was Hal Blaine, but he often used Earl. "Spector you could always get along with, if you didn't need him. If you needed him he was horrible. He wanted complete control. 'You've Lost That Lovin' Feelin'' took maybe three days to get right: a lot of double-scale money for me. Maybe on [Ike and Tina Turner's] 'River Deep Mountain High' I had a bit more freedom. That was a hell of a session, too—Phil threw Ike Turner out. Both of 'em had guns; I was thinking, 'Aw, why don't they shoot each other, they so bad?' When Ike first came to L.A. he insisted on paying cash. He didn't pay bad, just cash; he was used to dealing with people where he'd come in with a big sack of money. I said, 'I'm sorry, man, I can't do that.' He was somewhat belligerent about it. I said, 'Hey, just get somebody else.' 'Suppose I want you?' 'Well, you gonna have to make a contract.' 'Suppose I don't want to *make* no contract?' Somebody told me, 'Better cool it, this cat's got a pistol.' I said, 'Well, I'm sure he ain't got the last one made!' Damn right. I didn't carry no pistol, but Ike didn't have to know that. But I never had no real trouble with him. And regardless of what anyone might say, I'll tell you one thing: He made that girl's career."

The only early-Sixties alchemist more single-minded than Spector in turning R&B into pop was Motown Records. The company's artists were black, but its clever slogan was "The Sound of Young America": It was for everyone. Earl played on almost a decade's worth of Motown songs; earlier than people realize, Motown was using L.A. musicians. The players themselves were hardly aware of it. "There was a union rule in those days that the artist had to be in the studio. So we found ourselves playing behind these two girls, the Lewis Sisters, and they never had a release in their life! I'd hear a Temptations song on the radio and think, 'Damn, I never played with the Tempts, but that's me!' It turned out Motown was shipping our tracks back to Detroit and recutting the vocals. When the union found out, Motown had to pay us retroactive money.

"I broke with Motown in the early Seventies. They claimed to be 'the soul company' and it irked me that the highest-paid people in that company were not blacks. They'd heard me talkin' and had already backed off on calling me. I didn't care. Don't claim to be almighty black if you can't find no black people to do your business, and excuse me, but fuck y'all, don't call me no more. They're such hypocrites, Motown.

"In the original Motown sound, they didn't use any cymbals. The first few times I worked with them, I'd go to the cymbals and they'd say, 'No, no!' and I'd say, 'Oh, right, y'all don't like cymbals.' So I'd concentrate on the snare, and that related right back to New Orleans. Don't misunderstand me: It was [Motown drummer] Benny Benjamin who created that no-cymbal sound. Him and the bass player [James Jamerson] made the Motown Sound, them two guys and Wah-Wah Watson the guitar player. I knew Jamerson, we toured with Maria Muldaur, and I do believe he died of a broken heart from that first big TV special [NBC's "Motown 25," in 1983]. They mentioned every goddamn body connected with Motown but those two guys. Jamerson had stopped drinking, and he started again.

"But that's what tees me off about the Rock and Roll Hall of Fame. How many instrumentalists do you see in that? They couldn't ignore Dave Bartholomew, but who else is there? Not myself, not Benny Benjamin, not Jamerson. These guys started *sounds*, man; these guys locked singers in, singers that had some little song, sumbitches couldn't keep time in a basket.

"But when you talk about rock 'n' roll, you talkin' 'bout only one kind of music. In the Sixties I started turning down dates to prove a point, that I hadn't studied music for four years to play rock 'n' roll." The records Earl is proudest of aren't with rockers, but with Sarah Vaughan—"the greatest female vocalist of all time, outside opera." His small-band jazz albums, while not easy to find, are first-rate: a handful each with flutist Buddy Collette and guitarist Howard Roberts; 1958's wonderfully titled *Swingin' Flue in Hi-Fi* by the Strollers (Earl, Plas Johnson, and others) and Lalo Schifrin's 1982 *Ins and Outs*, on which Earl is especially good: muscular, smooth, and fast. Earl has toured with Schifrin, Peggy Lee, and Benny Carter, who once congratulated him on the best display of sight-reading Carter had ever heard from a drummer.

The West Coast's studios were clogged with brilliant musicians grinding away in obscurity. For Earl, "the most unsung of them all is [arranger] Ernie Freeman. A genius. He'd be drunk a whole week, write three, four albums, and know every damn note he wrote. I'd see him arrange for a thirty-piece orchestra, never sit down at the piano. Write a score like he was writin' a letter. When he died it was four, five days before anyone found him. The biggest hit Sinatra ever had, what was that? 'Strangers in the Night.' That's a pretty good example of Ernie's talent. And they never signed him up for any film work because he was black."

Nor has Earl ever been asked to produce an album, "even through I *came* here as an A&R man, which is what? A producer. Besides, who the fuck they think is running most of the fuckin' dates, excuse my language, while some little jackass producer don't know his ass from a hole in the ground is in the booth? The instrumentalists, that's who. Twenty years ago, [singer/keyboardist] Ronnie Barron told a Warners executive, I won't call his name, that he wanted me to produce his album. The guy said, 'Oh, Earl's a good drummer, but he can't produce.' He didn't even investigate to find out if I could. If I were white, it would've been 'Okay, let's give him a try.' I've been asked if people could borrow my drums because they like their sound. What the hell, they think the drums play themselves? I said, 'You really want 'em? Really? Okay. Cost you triple scale and cartage.' "

Lots of Earl's frustration is funneled into his new job. In the early Eighties his calls finally began to taper off ("Electronics is what fucked me up; if you're a drummer, you play what they consider drums and right now that's electronic drums"). So in 1982 he ran for, and won, the job of treasurer of the ten-thousand-member Local 47 of the American Federation of Musicians. Beaten in '84, he was reelected in 1990. He oversees what he refers to as "the company's" finances: membership, bookkeeping, computers. "It's a matter of doing something constructive based on the only life I know. If I can help a musician with his dues structure, that's great. I know how difficult it is out there. Anybody can come in and talk, if I'm not tied up. People come in and ask about drumming all the time, which is okay, that's helping 'em, too. *If* I'm not doin' anything. If I'm busy, I'm not there to give a drum lesson.

"I'll stay at the union the rest of my life, if I keep winning. If I don't, I'm retired. I don't think I'll ever go back to work as a drummer" (though he sits in almost nightly with jazz groups). "There's still a lot of places I'd like to go. But some of those, the reasons I once wanted to go aren't there anymore. I'd love to go to Tahiti and find me a little hut on the other side of the beach with a whole lot of beautiful young Tahitian girls, but what the hell am I going to do with them at sixty-seven?"

"What are you proudest of?"

"My kids."

"What music?"

"Hell, all of it. I've played good rock, good jazz, I've even played good polka, and I'm proud of it all. I'm proud of the respect I've achieved, whether I've got any *money* to show for it or not. I didn't expect to have any money; I was born poor. I'm glad I have the understanding to know why I'm not rich. I'm glad I'm not bitter about having experienced so many things that've been disadvantageous to me; that I'm not so bitter I couldn't teach my children that you deal with people on a one-on-one basis, you don't condemn any people as a whole. I'm proud I got that over to my children and that they're getting it over to their children. Because things *will* get better; I've seen them get better."

"Do you ever regret that you didn't spend your life playing jazz?"

"No. No, I don't. Because if I hadn't done what I did, which is the reason you interviewing me now, I don't think I'd have been more outstanding as a jazz drummer than any of the great jazz drummers from New Orleans we been talkin' about: Vernel Fournier, Eddie Blackwell, Charles Hungry Williams. It's nice to be recognized as special instead of just one of a bunch."

Earl patted his pockets. "God, I wanna cigarette. I quit, but if I don't take a drag now and then, I'll die of hypertension faster than I would from emphysema. I have withdrawal and get so frustrated. Talking to you today, I start feeling stupid not to remember things that are very important. It makes me sound blasé and I'm not, it's just that it's so damn long ago and there is so much of it."

"Call me 'round noon, I don't throw up till then" were his parting words after lunch, but when the rental car pulled up at one the next afternoon, Earl was in fine fettle despite having been out all night: ready to do the festival big-time. Headliners Los Lobos were booming from a big outdoor stage as Earl made straight for the jazz tent, rolling backstage like a southern diplomat, a world-champion hangout king prowling in and out of trailers, snagging hors d'oeuvres, roaring with laughter, hugging and waving; huddling with Nicholas Payton, the awesome seventeen-year-old trumpeter, and New Orleans jazz and R&B greats Harold Battiste, Earl Turbinton, and John Boudreaux; hailing with Ellis Marsalis with his fourteen-year-old son Jason. "Hey, Ellis, where's Dolores?" Sotto voce: "She's Ellis's wife, *fantastic* woman, a ramrod, kept those boys from getting a big head. Ellis and I are alike; we love to play a waltz."

The Dirty Dozen Brass Band were midset, threatening to levitate the jazz tent. A quiet, ironic voice said, "Hello, Mr. Palmer," and Earl wheeled around to face David Hidalgo of Los Lobos. "Hey!" hollered Earl. "I know this guy from when he hung around the union!" Hidalgo's bandmates Louie Perez and Steve Berlin arrived, fresh from their set, with an entourage of managers, friends, wives, and as everyone stood around watching the Dirty Dozen, the cultural resonances were dizzying: Here was Earl Palmer, waiting to hear the Dozen's version of the "Flintstones" theme he recorded thirty years ago, surrounded by the group whose only big hit is a remake of "La Bamba"—Earl Palmer on drums, 1959. Earl wasn't just standing there; his spirit presided. Hidalgo, in big black clodhoppers and ponytail, asked him what he'd used on Ritchie Valens's "Donna"—sticks? Brushes? "Closed brushes," said Earl.

Earl sat down. "I'm stressed out," he said. His comrade from the Fifties, bassist Chuck Badie, materialized in a beret and the two wandered into the food trailer. Munching a po' boy, Earl contemplated a hot-sauce bottle. Badie started to splutter. Earl burst into his raspy guffaw. "Badie, man, I had forgotten! Me and Badie, we'd get off from the Dew Drop at five, six in the morning and we'd go down to the Audubon Zoo. Chuck and I always wanted to hang out, everyone else went home. We would walk around the zoo at dawn smoking reefer, watching the monkeys clown. And the damn monkeys would throw their shit on us! So we went back to the Dew Drop, stole a bottle of hot sauce, sprinkled it on some peanuts, and fed 'em to the monkeys. They started squeakin', hoppin' up and down, runnin' around. *But they kept eating the peanuts!* Even though it was drivin' 'em crazy!" The two gray-haired men were knock-kneed with laughter, wiping their eyes, holding each other up. "That's why," Earl gasped, "when they say you're as dumb as a monkey—man, you dumb!"

"Birks [Dizzy Gillespie] is somethin'. I did a Monterey Jazz All-Stars thing with him and Gil Fuller's big band. He said, 'You unique.'

"I said, 'Thank you, Birks!'

"He said, 'Ain't talkin' 'bout your fuckin' playing —'

" 'Well, *fuck* you, then!'

" ' — I'm talkin' 'bout that cymbal. I like that one. You wanna give it to me?' Birks, he would carry a cymbal around and give it to drummers: 'Here, use this.' "

The cymbal Dizzy admired was an old Zildjian "that sounded like shit until I put rivets in it, then it was the best rivet cymbal I ever heard." In his New Orleans years Earl played a basic Gretsch kit: two mounted toms, one floor tom, snare, bass and fourteen-inch hi-hat. Later he added Ludwig, Rogers, Camco, and Yamaha kits; the Rogers set had two mounted toms, thirteen and fourteen inches. Except for one Paiste ride, his cymbals have always been Zildjians. His current drums are "a little Ludwig kit I can put in my car": snare, twenty-inch bass, thirteen- and fourteen-inch mounted toms, sixteen-inch floor tom, twenty-inch Zildjian ride, seventeen-inch Paiste ride, eighteen-inch Zildjian sizzle, and fourteen-inch hi-hat.

January 1992

240